Coaching Soccer Effectively

The American Coaching Effectiveness Program
Level 1 Soccer Book

Coaching Soccer Effectively

The American Coaching Effectiveness Program
Level 1 Soccer Book

Christopher A. Hopper, PhD
Humboldt State University

Michael S. Davis, PhD
Mount Hood Community College

Human Kinetics Books
Champaign, Illinois

Library of Congress Cataloging-in-Publication Data
Hopper, Christopher, A., 1952-
    Coaching soccer effectively.
    Includes index.
    1.   Soccer—Coaching.   I. Davis, Michael S.,
1945-   II. Title.
GV943.8.H65   1988   796.334'07'7   86-34268
ISBN 0-87322-112-5

Developmental Editors: Steven Houseworth and Linda Anne Bump
Assistant Editors: Janet Beals and JoAnne Cline
Production Director: Ernie Noa
Projects Manager: Lezli Harris
Text Design: Keith Blomberg
Typesetter: Yvonne Winsor
Illustrations: Dick Flood
Cover Design and Layout: Jack Davis
Printed by: Phillips Brothers

ISBN: 0-87322-112-5

Printed in the United States of America

10 9 8 7 6 5 4 3 2 1

Human Kinetics Books
A Division of Human Kinetics Publishers, Inc.
Box 5076
Champaign, IL 61820
1-800-DIAL-HKP
1-800-334-3665 (In Illinois)

Series Preface

Coaching Soccer Effectively is part of the American Coaching Effectiveness Program (ACEP) Level 1 sport-specific series. The decision to produce this series evolved after the release of the ACEP Level 1 sport science course. In that course local youth sport administrators were encouraged to apply the information presented to the specific sports in their program. They were asked to identify the skills to be taught and the proper progression in teaching these skills. They were also asked to develop a seasonal plan and sample practice plans for their coaches.

The task seemed easy enough, but it was not. Considerable time is needed to carefully identify the skills to be taught and then to put them into a seasonal plan from which daily practice plans can be derived. As a result, the ACEP staff were encouraged to develop this information for various sports, which we now have done.

The ACEP LEVEL 1 sport-specific series is unique in several ways.

1. The emphasis is on *teaching* skills to athletes, not on how to learn the skills yourself, as in most other books.
2. The emphasis also is on teaching basic skills to beginning athletes. Often, they will be very young children, but not always. Therefore, the books in this series are developed for coaches who teach the basics to children from 6 to 15 years of age.
3. Careful consideration is given to the proper *progression* for teaching these skills. Information from the field of motor development is combined with the practical experience of veteran coaches to ensure that the progressions maximize learning and minimize the risk of injury.
4. *Seasonal* plans for the teaching of basic skills are presented along with *daily practice plans* for three age groups. Coaches will find these plans very helpful.
5. Drills or exercises appropriate for beginning athletes are also included.

Three other helpful features appear in each book in this series: A short history of the sport to help you appreciate the evolution of the game, a glossary of terms, and the rules of the sport are provided.

PRACTICAL, BASIC, and ACCURATE were the guiding principles in preparing this series. The content had to be practical for beginning coaches and yet equally useful for more experienced coaches. Coaches did not need another treatise on the sport; many of those are already available.

Keeping this series basic was perhaps the most difficult task. Including more information about the skills to impress coaches with all the knowledge available was constantly tempting. However, we resisted because this is not what coaches of beginning athletes need.

Finally, accuracy was essential; thus, many expert coaches and sport scientists reviewed the content of the book to confirm its accuracy.

To achieve maximum benefit, the books in this series cannot be read in an evening and then be put aside. They must be used like a reference book, a dictionary, or a working manual. Read

v

the book thoroughly; then refer to it often during the season.

This book and ACEP are dedicated to the purpose of improving the quality of youth sports. We hope you will find the books in the series useful to you in achieving that goal. Enjoy your coaching, and thanks for helping young people learn to play sports better.

Rainer Martens, PhD
ACEP Founder

Contents

List of Drills and Activities

Preface

This book is dedicated to helping you become a more effective soccer coach. Besides knowledge of the game, effective coaching depends on the ability to understand children and youths, plan learning experiences, communicate effectively, motivate players, and analyze and correct performances. This book combines these abilities with practical coaching information, which describes skills and tactics and shows you how to teach them to your players using various drills and games. We have included only those drills and games that are effective and enjoyable for children.

Coaching Soccer Effectively is a collection of soccer coaching information that is based on our combined total of over 30 years of practical coaching experience at youth, high school, college, and professional levels. The book will be particularly useful for those of you who coach players between the ages of 6 and 15.

We designed the book as a unique coaching and teaching tool, which identifies the components of the game and provides specific strategies for implementation in practice and games. The first part of the book explains how to teach fundamental skills of the game by emphasizing coaching points and developing practices through a series of progressive steps from simple drills to game practice. The second part of the book examines the tactical aspects of the game by introducing simple tactical concepts and illustrating how to teach those concepts to players to create a cohesive team. This section will also assist you in identifying those talents that individual players need for successful performance in specific positions.

Finally the book helps you organize your coaching with well-designed seasonal plans. This allows you to plan successful learning experiences in soccer for your players. As well as providing you with well-organized and proven practices, this book is based on the theme of enjoyment for both you and your team. Soccer is one of the world's greatest and most popular sports because it is enjoyable. Reflecting on our former coaches, we realized that those who made practice and games enjoyable were the most effective. We pass our ideas and experiences in coaching soccer on to you in hopes that they will allow you to enjoy the game as much as we do.

In closing, we would like to thank John Hannigan, Eric Mild, Kiley Simmons, and Nike shoes for their assistance in the preparation of the original photographs from which much of the artwork included in the book was developed.

Chris Hopper

Mike Davis

Soccer Coaching Guide

Welcome to soccer! Your interest in coaching young athletes will be rewarded in many ways throughout the soccer season. You will experience the joy of seeing young players learn and develop skills, establish new friendships, develop confidence, win games, and thoroughly enjoy playing soccer. However, you also will need to discipline players from time to time, deal with parents who may become too emotionally involved in their child's activity, and you may need to check your emotions from time to time. The information presented in this Coaching Guide will help you understand how to teach soccer skills and playing strategies effectively so that you can maximize your joy and minimize your frustration. If you are determined to help the beginning players on your team have a positive and successful soccer experience, and if you take the time to study *Coaching Soccer Effectively*, then you will be on your way to a successful season.

However, before you jump into learning how to teach soccer, take some time to consider how you will approach the players on your team and the general atmosphere you want to create during practices and games. As a coach, establishing your coaching philosophy before the season begins is very important. You need to decide (a) your goals, or what you want to accomplish, and (b) how you will accomplish these goals. You may want to consider one of two major coaching philosophies: You might choose to emphasize winning as the most important objective, or you might stress participation, fun, and skill development as the most important objectives.

The philosophy advocated through the American Coaching Effectiveness Program is *Athletes First—Winning Second*. This means that every decision you make as a coach should first be in the best interest of your athletes, and second in the desire to win. Hopefully, helping young people to develop physically, psychologically, and socially will always be more important to you than beating the other team.

Athletes First—Winning Second does not mean winning is unimportant, or said more accurately, that striving to win is unimportant. You should instill in your players a desire to win, to do their best, to pursue excellence. However, the outcome of the game—the winning or losing—is not the most important objective. The most important objective is that your players try to win, that they try their best. If they do their best, they will have been successful—regardless of the outcome of the contest.

This philosophy also will be reflected in how you present yourself to the players on your team. As a coach, you are in an influential position. Thus, *how* you teach will be as important as what you teach. To implement the ACEP philosophy, consider the following points:

Be a good role model. Present a model for behavior you want your athletes to emulate. Set positive examples at practices and games.

Everyone is important. Treat each player as an important human being. Each player will have a different personality and different needs. Be sensitive to these differences and show interest and concern for each team member.

Consider the age and skill levels of your players. Your athletes will be full of energy and eager to try many skills. However, they are also young and not yet capable of performing as adults. This means you must approach your athletes at their level. Do not expect them to come up to your level.

Consider individual differences. Teach beginning soccer skills according to the ability of each player. Some players will be fast learners with whom you can progress rapidly. Other players will not learn as quickly, so you will need to proceed more slowly with them.

Keep everyone active. Organize your practices and games so that each player is able to participate as much as possible. Young players want to play soccer for many reasons; one of the most important reasons is to have fun participating. If they are not kept active in practices or allowed to play in games, they will quickly lose interest.

Include athletes in the decision-making process. Young athletes should have input as to what skills they practice and as to how they practice them. Ask your players what they need to work on, how they want to be grouped for practice, and what positions they would like to play. Naturally, young athletes should not control the entire practice, but do consider their interests and ideas when designing practices and playing games.

Be patient. You will need to have patience with beginning players who are learning soccer. Soccer skills require coordination that can only be developed through repeated practice. Encourage your players to develop their skills, and positively reinforce players for their effort and skill development. When young players learn new skills, both you and your players should be proud.

Part I:
The Basics

Your players will enjoy kicking balls, dribbling, and shooting. But your players must also be prepared to experience having the ball stolen and having shots blocked. Helping your players develop realistic goals about their offensive and defensive achievements is as important as teaching them basic skills. Also, because soccer will be a new game to most of your players you will need to introduce soccer to them.

This section presents an explanation of soccer and how to teach individual offensive and defensive skills. The coaching points, teaching progressions, illustrations, and practice activities will help you understand and plan how to teach and how to develop these skills.

The following key will help you in interpreting the drill diagrams:

$- - \rightarrow$ players movement without the ball
$\longrightarrow$ movement of the ball
$\sim\!\!\sim\!\!\rightarrow$ player dribbling the ball

Chapter 1: The Game of Soccer

Introduction: The World's Most Popular Game

Soccer is the most popular game in the world and is played in virtually every country. Soccer has the largest world championship of any sport, a spectacular soccer superbowl called the World Cup that attracts millions of spectators. Every four years the very best teams in the world play each other for the World Cup. No other sporting event draws such worldwide interest.

Soccer is a relatively new game in the United States, but elsewhere people have played soccer for hundreds of years. Soccer originated in England during the Middle Ages. At that time soccer was played between villages with the whole population of each village playing as a team. A round object was kicked several miles between each village. Few rules existed in the medieval games, but later England became the first country to establish playing rules and a governing body of soccer, the English Football Association. Yes, that's right, in England soccer is called "football," and the game remains known as football in every country except the United States. The international governing body of soccer is the Fédération Internationale de Football Association (FIFA).

Soccer is different from traditional American sports because players use the feet and head but not the hands to pass the ball and score goals. The only exception to this rule is the goal-keepers, who can use their hands to stop shots and to pass the ball. As your players will learn, keeping possession of the ball with the feet is not easy and requires considerable foot-eye coordination.

Soccer is a team game with 11 players on each team. The object of the game is to score points by kicking the ball into the opposing team's goal. Soccer is an active game with few rules, plenty of running and action, and fun for everyone on the field. Thus in recent years it has become a very popular participant sport with a broad base of support from people of all ages.

Much of the fun in soccer develops because the transition from offense to defense is constant and play continues when a team loses possession of the ball. The field is large enough that the ball does not go out of play for several minutes, and players must constantly change from offense to defense. The clock runs continuously, and once the game has started, coaches must let the players play and make decisions. No time-outs are permitted except in case of injury. You may shout instructions to players from the sideline, but constant chatter can distract players who are trying to play a game that demands their undivided attention.

Field of Play

The soccer field is rectangular, and its exact dimensions depend on the regulations of the soccer league or governing body. In international matches the maximum size of the field is 130 yd long by 80 yd wide, but fields are rarely that large. Fields for college and high school play are usually between 100 and 120 yd long and between 50 and 75 yd wide. Fields for youth players should be smaller than fields for adults. The field is often called the *pitch* and is marked with boundary lines as shown in Figure 1-1. The lines running the length of the pitch are the *touchlines* or *sidelines*, and the lines running at the end of the pitch are the *goal lines* or *endlines*.

A goal 8 ft high and 8 yd wide is placed in the middle of the goal line, but smaller goals are suggested for players under 12. A goal net should be attached to the back of the goal to catch the ball when a goal is scored. Portable goals are recommended because they can be moved around a field to save wear and tear on the grass in front of the goalmouth.

Fig. 1-1

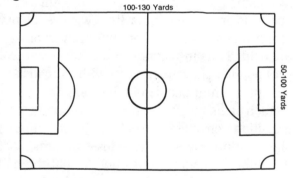

100-130 Yards

50-100 Yards

We recommend the following field sizes and goal modifications for younger players:

Age of Players	Goal Size	Field Size
6-8	6 ft high	70 yd long
	6 yd wide	50 yd wide
9-11	7 ft high	80 yd long
	7 yd wide	55 yd wide

Field Markings

A soccer field is marked to designate areas of play. Field markings specify the areas around a

goal, the field of play from out-of-bounds, where play begins, and where goal kicks and corner kicks are taken.

Markings Around Each Goal

The *goal area* is a rectangular space in front of each goal that begins 6 yd beyond each goalpost on the goal line and extends 6 yd out into the field of play. The ball is placed inside this area when goal kicks are taken. The *penalty area* is a large rectangular area in front of each goal inside of which lies the goal area. The penalty area begins 18 yd beyond each goalpost on the goal line and extends 18 yd into the field of play; this is the area in which the goalkeeper can handle the ball. The *penalty spot* is a mark 12 yd from the midpoint of the goal line from which a *penalty kick* is taken. Penalty kicks are awarded when the defensive team commits a direct free-kick foul inside the penalty area. *The penalty area arc* is a 10-yd arc drawn at the top of the penalty area from the penalty spot. During a penalty kick, all players except the penalty kicker must be outside the penalty area and the penalty arc. This rule ensures that all players are at least 10 yd from the ball.

Markings at the Center

The *center circle* is in the middle of the field with a radius of 10 yd from the exact center of the field, which is called the *center spot*. A kickoff is taken from the center spot to begin the game and to resume play after a goal has been scored. On kickoffs all opposing players must remain 10 yd from the ball in their own half of the field or outside the center circle. The *halfway line* divides the field into two halves and is marked by a flag set back from the sideline. Players must be in their own halves of the field at the kickoff, but after the kickoff players can run anywhere on the field to receive the ball.

Markings at the Corners

A flag is placed at each corner of the field where the touchline and goal line intersect. At each corner there is a 1-yd radius arc where the ball is placed for a *corner kick*. A corner kick from the corner arc is awarded to the offensive team if the defensive team kicks the ball beyond the goal line.

Players

Each team consists of 11 players, one of whom is the goalkeeper. Each team needs 7 players to start the game. As with field size, the number of players on a team is determined by the soccer league or governing body. In international games, teams are allowed to name 5 substitutes but may use only 2 of them. At the youth level, teams normally consist of between 13 and 18 players and substitution is freely permitted. For a simplified game, young teams often play with 7, 8, or 9 players on a side. Players are arranged into positions, with a goalkeeper, defensive players, midfielders, and forwards or strikers (see Figure 1-2).

Fig. 1-2

Goalkeeper

Because the goalkeeper's main job is to prevent the ball from going into the goal, the goalkeeper is the only player allowed to use the hands. But even the goalkeeper may use the hands only inside the penalty area. The goalkeeper provides his or her team's last line of defense, and any mistake the goalkeeper makes is costly to the team. Thus a goalkeeper must be agile, have a strong pair of hands, and understand soccer tactics. Because the goalkeeper often initiates the offense, he or she should be able to kick and throw the ball both powerfully and accurately. Instead of merely getting rid of the ball, a goalkeeper should think in terms of setting up the offense.

Defensive Players

Teams generally play with four defensive players, including two outside fullbacks and two central defensive players. The objective of these four players is to win the ball from opponents and to prevent the opponents from creating shooting opportunities. Defensive players also play an important role in offensive play, however, by moving the ball up the field after stealing the ball or after receiving the ball from the goalkeeper. Defenders can also be used in offensive strategies. For example, a defensive player who is a good header can be used to create shots from corner kicks.

Midfielders

Midfielders are the link players between the forwards and the defense. They are generally all-purpose players who have good endurance and can play both offense and defense. Midfielders are important because the team that dominates the midfield is likely to control the game. Depending on their system of play, teams may elect to play with two, three, or four midfielders; most teams opt for three.

Forwards or Strikers

Forwards play nearest the opponents' goal and are the primary offensive players. Teams usually play with two, three, or four forwards, two of whom are called *wings* and play near the sidelines. The remaining forwards play in the center and are called *central forwards*. Wings usually advance the ball up the side and, when near the goal, pass to the center.

Players' Equipment

Soccer requires little equipment, but your athletes should know how they are expected to dress. Also, you will need to inform your players and their parents of the *proper* equipment to ensure safety and to reduce the potential for injury.

Footwear

Shoes are a soccer player's most important piece of equipment. Soccer shoes should fit comfortably and snugly to enable players to develop a "feel" for the ball. Advise players to select shoes according to the surface on which they will play. Shorter, multistudded, molded shoes are suitable for most grass surfaces, but longer, detachable cleats work well on wet grass or loose surfaces. Flat-soled shoes work best on synthetic outdoor surfaces and indoor gym floors.

Shirt and Shorts

Players' clothes should be appropriate for the current weather. In warm weather short-sleeved shirts and lightweight shorts are desirable. In cold weather players should wear long-sleeved shirts and shorts of heavier, warmer material. Because players need to move freely, they should wear clothes that fit comfortably and are neither too tight nor too loose.

Shin Guards and Socks

Shin guards are an essential piece of equipment that fit between the sock and leg to protect the shins from kicks. Shin guards are lightweight, inexpensive, and easy to wear. We recommend wearing long, knee-length socks to further protect the leg from kicks, to hold shin guards in place, and to keep the lower legs warm.

Goalkeepers' Special Attire

Goalkeepers wear a different colored jersey from the field players to help distinguish them from players who cannot handle the ball. Goalies can wear shirts with padding at the elbows and shorts with padding at the hips to help cushion falls. Additional elbow and knee pads can also be worn. In cold weather, goalkeepers should wear gloves, a warm undershirt, and long sweat pants. In wet weather, gloves made from leather with rubber pimples will help to grip the ball firmly.

Balls

Soccer balls are made in three sizes. Size 3 is the smallest and is used for young players under age 7. Players aged 7 to 12 should use a Size 4 ball, which is also used to play indoor soccer. We recommend a Size 5 ball for players over 12 years of age. One ball should be available for every player so that he or she can develop individual skills. These balls need not be expensive but should be durable enough for players to practice. Just as many youngsters improvise broomsticks for bats and soft drink cans for basketballs, soccer players can use about anything that rolls or slides. In fact, the famous Brazilian player Pelé practiced with a grapefruit!

Officials

Officials are an important part of soccer because they organize and conduct the game according to the rules. In fact, without officials there would be no game. In some youth soccer leagues, officials are adult or student volunteers who may not have formal training. In other leagues, officials are qualified according to state and national standards.

Officials are human and make mistakes just like players. Although you and your players may disagree with calls, try to remain positive and calmly ask officials about those calls after the game. Your games may be officiated by two officials or by three officials, and it will help you to understand how officials position themselves. In a *two-official system*, the referees move diagonally across the field and each official is responsible for one half of the field (see Figure 1-3). In a *three-official system*, one referee controls the field and two linesmen assist by patrolling opposite sidelines (see Figure 1-4).

Fig. 1-3

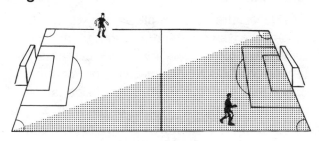

Fig. 1-4

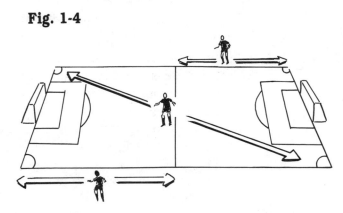

Control of the game is the responsibility of the referee, who disciplines players for misconduct. Players who foul opponents intentionally or who are abusive are shown a yellow card as a first warning. A second violation results in a red card or ejection from the game. The referee can choose, however, to eject a player at the first misconduct or violation. Ejected players cannot be replaced by a substitute; thus the team plays one player short. All calls by referees are judgment calls, and players and coaches should respect the judgment of the referee rather than complain about calls and badger referees.

How the Game Starts and Proceeds

At the beginning of the game, choice of ends and kickoff are decided by the toss of a coin. The team winning the toss can decide to kickoff or choose which end of the field to play. The player taking the kickoff must pass the ball forward so

that it rolls its circumference, as shown in Figure 1-5, and cannot touch the ball again until it has been touched by another player. At the kickoff all players must be in their own half of the field. After a goal has been scored and at the beginning of the second half, the game is resumed by a kickoff. At the start of the second half, the teams change ends, and the team that did not kick off in the first half kicks off the second half. We recommend the following time periods for each age group:

Age of Players	Game Length	Half Time
Adults	Two 45-min halves	15 min
Under 19	Two 45-min halves	15 min
Under 16	Two 40-min halves	15 min
Under 14	Two 35-min halves	10 min
Under 12	Two 30-min halves	10 min
Under 10	Two 25-min halves	10 min
Under 8	Two 20-min halves	10 min

Overtime periods may be played in some competitions depending on league or governing body rules.

Fig. 1-5

Ball In and Out of Play

The ball is *out of play* only when the entire ball crosses over the touchline or goal line. If part of the ball is still covering the line, the ball is in play. Unlike in football or basketball, in soccer players can stand out of bounds and play a ball in bounds (see Figure 1-6). For a goal to be scored, the entire ball must cross the line between the goalposts. When the ball passes over the touchlines or sidelines, the team that last touched the ball before it went out of bounds loses possession, and the opposing team is awarded a throw-in. If the defensive team kicks the ball over the endline, the offensive team receives a corner kick. If the offensive team kicks the ball over the endline, the game is restarted with a goal kick.

Fig. 1-6

Fouls

Fouls are divided into two types: *major* and *minor*. Major fouls result in a *direct free kick*, and minor fouls result in an *indirect free kick*. Indirect free kicks must be touched by another player before a goal can be scored. Direct free kicks can be shot directly at the goal. The following list presents offenses that result in direct or indirect free kicks:

Direct Free Kick	*Indirect Free Kick*
Handling the ball	Dangerous play
Kicking an opponent	Obstruction
Striking an opponent	Goalkeeper taking too many steps
Tripping an opponent	Offside
Holding an opponent	
Pushing an opponent	
Jumping at an opponent	
Charging an opponent	
Charging from behind	
Unsportsmanlike conduct	

Offside

Offside occurs when a player passes the ball toward the goal to a teammate and there are not two defending players (one defender plus the goalkeeper) between the receiving player and the opponents' goal (see Figure 1-7). Offside can only occur in the opponents' half of the field, and a player is only offside when the referee rules that the player is interfering with play. A player cannot be offside directly from a goal kick, corner kick, throw-in, or drop ball nor when the ball is played backward.

Fig. 1-7

WILL BE OFFSIDE IF RECEIVES THE BALL

Restarting the Game

Restarts, or resuming the game after play has stopped, are common in soccer, and play resumes quickly because the clock does not stop. Referees only stop the clock if a serious injury delays play or if a team deliberately tries to waste time. Teaching your team how to take restarts is an important part of coaching soccer effectively, because your team has an opportunity to keep possession of the ball or create a scoring opportunity.

Drop Ball

A *drop ball* is given after the referee stops the game due to an injury to a player. The referee drops the ball between two opposing players who contest for the ball after it touches the ground. A dropped ball must touch the ground before it is kicked by either player.

Penalty Kick

A *penalty kick* is awarded to the offensive team if the defensive team commits a direct free kick offense within the penalty area. The kick is taken from the penalty spot by any player on the offensive team, usually a player who is cool under pressure and a very accurate shooter. The goalkeeper is the only defensive player allowed to try to stop the kick. The goalkeeper's heels must be on the goal line, and the goalkeeper may not move until the kick is taken and all other players (offensive and defensive) are 10 yd from the ball, outside the penalty area, and outside the penalty arc as shown in Figure 1-8.

Fig. 1-8

Corner Kick

When the defensive team kicks the ball beyond the goal line, the offensive team is awarded a *corner kick*. Opposing players must be at least 10 yd away when the kick is taken, but offensive

players can stand as close as they want to the kicker. As shown in Figures 1-9 and 1-10, the usual strategy is to cross the ball into the goal-mouth for a shot or a header at the goal, or a short pass from the corner is made to teammates who then try to pass or shoot.

Fig. 1-9

Fig. 1-10

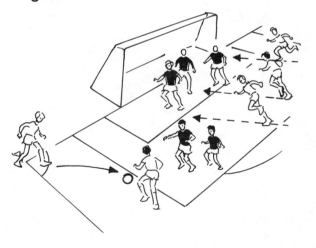

Goal Kick

A *goal kick* is awarded to the opposing team when an offensive player kicks the ball over the goal line without the ball going into the goal. The defensive team places the ball within the goal area on the same side of the goal from which the ball went out of play. The ball must pass outside the penalty area before it is in play, and any player on the team can take the kick. Normally, however, the kick is taken by the goalkeeper because, if one of your field players takes the goal kick, then one less player is available to receive a pass.

Throw-In

All of your players should learn how to take throw-ins because the ball often goes out of play over the touchlines and every player must be ready to throw the ball in play quickly. The team last touching the ball loses possession, and the other team gains the ball. When taking a throw-in, both feet must stay in contact with the ground and part of each foot must be behind the touch-line (see Figure 1-11). The thrower must use both hands and deliver the ball from behind the head in one continuous movement. After the ball has been thrown onto the field, another player must touch the ball before the thrower can play it

again. If the thrower makes an illegal or foul throw, the ball is given to the other team to throw in. A goal cannot be scored directly from a throw-in.

Fig. 1-11

Chapter 2: Passing and Support Play

Introduction: The Basis of Soccer Play

As in all team sports where the objective is to move the ball from one end to the other in order to score, advancing and controlling the ball are essential to effective soccer play. The fastest way to advance the ball is to pass from one teammate to another. Thus learning specific passes is extremely important. Players must also learn to position themselves to receive passes and utilize specific skills in receiving passes, or even the most technically perfect passes will be ineffective. Thus learning how to receive passes and *support* the ball are also important.

In teaching soccer skills, passing and supporting the ball cannot be separated from receiving passes and controlling the ball. Like basketball players, soccer players must develop both passing skills and receiving skills to advance and control the ball effectively. In addition to technically correct and accurate passes, however, effective soccer play requires good support from teammates. This means that all soccer players must think about moving into positions where they can receive passes or support the ball. Passing and supporting the ball are the basis of effective soccer play. Thus we will present how to teach these skills first. In this chapter we will describe how to teach your players to pass and to support each other. How to actually present these complementary skills in practices is described in

chapter 13 on "Instructional Schedules and Practice Plans."

Teaching these team-playing concepts to young, inexperienced players is not easy. Thus you must approach your players at a level they can understand. Because young children have difficulty understanding the concept of teamwork, we recommend that you focus more on individual skills, movement basics, and enjoyment for players between 6 and 9 years. Players 10 years and older will be able to develop and integrate individual playing skills with teamwork, but this material should be more basic for younger than for older players. The following topics are presented in this chapter to help you teach players passing and support play:

- Passing Fundamentals
- Supporting Fundamentals
- Using Specific Passes
- Teaching Progression for Passing and Support Play
- Games and Activities for Passing and Support Play

Passing Fundamentals

Effective passing involves more than simply aiming and kicking the ball. Your players need to understand how to control their passes by kicking them in certain ways with the different surfaces of their feet. Thus, be sure to teach your players the fundamentals of where to kick the ball and how to pass the ball.

Where to Kick the Ball

Before setting up a passing practice for your players, introduce the soccer ball to them and demonstrate what will happen when they kick it. As shown in Figure 2-1, the soccer ball can be divided along the vertical plane and along the horizontal plane. Tell your players that if they kick the ball in the center or on the vertical plane, the ball will travel straight ahead. If they kick the ball on the right side, it will travel to the left; if they kick it on the left side, it will travel to the right.

Fig. 2-1

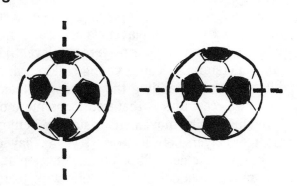

Then demonstrate that if they kick under the ball or below the horizontal plane, the ball will lift in the air but that if they kick it in the middle or on the top the ball will roll on the ground.

How to Pass the Ball

Once your players understand how the ball can be kicked in different directions, show them how to pass the ball by using (a) the *inside* of the foot, (b) the *instep* or *laces*, and (c) the *outside* of the foot (see Figure 2-2).

Explain that the greater the surface of the foot used to kick the ball, the better they can control the ball. Therefore, passing with the inside of the foot allows greater accuracy than passing with the instep or with the outside of the foot, because more of the foot contacts the ball.

Fig. 2-2

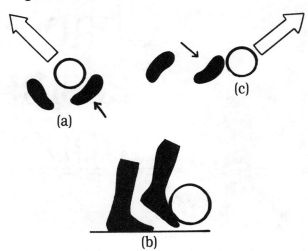

Also explain that the nonkicking foot and position of the body are important to passing correctly. As shown in Figure 2-3, the nonkicking foot should be placed alongside the ball. As the ball is kicked, the head moves over the ball. Demonstrate that it is easier to kick in the direction of the nonkicking foot, therefore your players should point the nonkicking foot in the direction of the target.

Fig. 2-3

Of course, the foot position is different for each of these passing styles. As shown in Figure 2-4, players should kick with the inside of the foot by placing the lead foot beside the ball with the toe pointing at the target, turning out the kicking foot and leg, and swinging toward the target.

Passing with the instep or laces is similar except that the toes of the kicking foot are turned down (see Figure 2-5). Passing with the outside of the foot may seem quite awkward, because it is not a natural style. Turn the foot down and point the toes in, as shown in Figure 2-6. Players should place the lead foot beside the ball and swing the leg toward the target. Many young players tend to stop the kick after contacting the ball. Therefore, you must explain that they should kick *through* the ball and follow through or extend the leg, as shown in Figure 2-7. Also, most beginning players will pass with their dominant foot only, but they should learn to pass with either foot. You can encourage the development of passing with each foot through drills.

Fig. 2-4

Fig. 2-5

Fig. 2-6

Fig. 2-7

To practice these passing skills, pair up your players with one ball per pair and have them practice the Passing Through Cones Drill (2.1), passing on the ground with each kicking surface. Ask them to notice what happens when the ball goes straight and when it goes astray. These subtle reminders will help your players to develop their passing skills. Other drills to help players practice passing are the Passing Against a Wall Drill (2.2), Knocking Over Cones (2.3), Marbles (2.4), and Passing Circle (2.5).

Coaching Points for Passing Fundamentals

1. Pass on the ground by kicking at the center or top of ball.
2. Pass in the air by kicking under the ball.
3. Place the nonkicking foot alongside and slightly behind the ball, pointing toward the target.
4. Pass with the inside of the foot by turning out the kicking leg and swinging toward the target. Use both the left foot as well as the right foot.
5. Pass with the instep by pointing the toes down and swinging toward the target.
6. Pass with the outside of the foot by placing the outside of the kicking foot on the ball and pushing toward the target.

Supporting Fundamentals

Supporting teammates means that each player should move into position to receive passes from the teammate with the ball. This means that your players must be able to recognize when they are in position to receive passes and when they are not in position to receive passes. Explain that to support his or her teammates, a player must move away from defensive players. As shown in Figure 2-8, the offensive players without the ball are positioned behind defensive players, and the ball would probably be stolen if passed to them. These players are not in position to support the teammate with the ball. As shown in Figure 2-9, however, the offensive players without the ball have now moved away from the defensive players and can receive passes from the teammate with the ball. If the defensive players follow these offensive players, they can simply continue to move to open areas of the field where the player with the ball can pass to them.

Fig. 2-8

Fig. 2-9

Demonstrate to your players that they can move into position to receive passes and to support the ball by (a) moving to the side and away from defensive players or (b) moving toward the ball and away from defensive players (see Figure 2-10).

Fig. 2-10

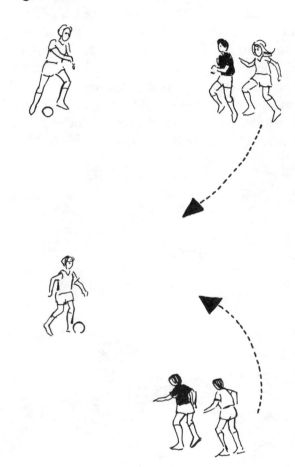

Using Specific Passes

After your players have learned the fundamentals of passing, teach them how specific passes are used in various situations. Of course, the passes you teach will depend on the age, skill level, and experience of your players. For younger, less experienced players, stick to *short, low passes*. For older, more experienced players, add *long, lofted passes*, *chip passes*, and *bent* or *curved passes*.

Short, Low Passes

Short passes on the ground are easier to control and easier for teammates to receive than long passes through the air. Short, low passes are effective for moving the ball between defenders quickly. Your players will be able to make short, low passes quite easily. Their greatest problem will be inconsistency, kicking the ball too soft or too hard.

Long, Lofted Passes

Sometimes your players will need to kick the ball over a long distance, either to a teammate far away or to clear the ball from the defense. Instruct your players to use long, lofted passes to advance the ball over long distances. Demonstrate that the proper method for lofting the ball is to (a) approach the ball from a slight angle, (b) swing the leg, and (c) kick under the ball with the instep or laces (see Figure 2-11). A good coaching hint to help loft the ball is to lean back slightly as the ball is kicked. For this pass, then, the head should be not over the ball but *behind* it to help shift the body weight back to raise the leg and loft the ball.

Fig. 2-11

Chip Passes and Shots

Sometimes your players will need to *chip* the ball a moderate distance over defenders. Chipping is an advanced skill and requires much practice to perfect. Explain and demonstrate that chips are similar to long, lofted passes except that the kick-

ing leg should stop short of a full follow-through (see Figure 2-12), causing the ball to rise quickly but not to travel far. Demonstrating how to kick under the ball, as if cutting the grass with the cleats, will help your players to develop a "feel" for chipping the ball.

Fig. 2-12

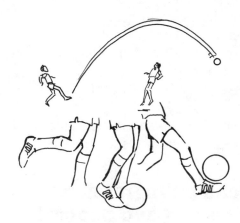

Bent or Curved Passes

Another way to pass the ball around defenders is to kick it slightly off center and follow through to one side, causing it to spin and curve in the air. Curving passes is similar to kicking long, lofted passes except that the ball is kicked off to the side. Demonstrate that to curve passes to the left, players must kick the ball underneath and follow through on the right side and that to curve passes to the right they must kick the ball underneath and follow through on the left side (see Figure 2-13). This is another advanced skill and should only be taught to experienced players who have mastered the other passes.

Fig. 2-13

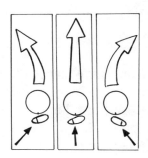

Coaching Points for Using Specific Passes

1. Use short, low passes to maintain possession of the ball and move it quickly between defenders.
2. Use long, lofted passes to move the ball long distances quickly.
3. Lean back and "cut" the grass under the ball with the cleats to help lift the ball off the ground.
4. Curve the ball by following through to the side of the ball.
5. Use chip passes to loft the ball short distances.
6. Use bent or curved passes to pass the ball in a curve around players.

Teaching Progressions for Passing and Support Play

1. Teach players how to contact the ball at the center, at the sides, underneath, and in the middle.
2. Teach players how to move away from defenders to open areas where they can receive passes and support teammates with the ball.
3. Teach players how to pass with the inside, top, and outside of the foot. Emphasize kicking with the left foot as well as with the right foot.
4. Teach players (a) short, low passes, (b) long, lofted passes, (c) chip passes, and (d) bent or curved passes.

Games and Activities for Passing and Support Play

After your players have learned these passing techniques, they will need to practice using them in two different settings. First, let your players play drills that are fun and that emphasize individual skill development. Second, after your players can pass and support each other fairly well, let them practice drills that simulate competitive or game situations. Drills 2.1 to 2.11 emphasize the development of individual passing skills and techniques. Drills 2.12 and 2.13 emphasize the development of individual skills and the application of these skills in competitive situations against opponents, simulating game conditions. Additional passing drills that simulate game conditions are 6.6, 9.4, 9.5, and 9.6. Practicing in competitive situations after developing individual skills is important, because passing skill involves not only accuracy but (a) disguising passes, (b) judging the speed and positioning of opponents, and (c) developing a feel for the speed, power, and placement of passes to teammates between defenders. By using the drills listed here and others with which you are familiar, you can guide the development of your players by applying the amount of defensive pressure against which your players are able to play effectively.

(2.1) Passing Through Cones

Purpose. To practice passes and passing accuracy.

Organization. Pair up players, with one ball per pair. Place two cones 3 to 4 ft apart about 10 ft from each player.

Directions. Players practice passing the ball through the cones. Older players can place the cones closer together. As players become more proficient, have them take a step back each time they pass through the cones. If you cannot use cones, have one partner spread his or her legs and alternate passing through the legs. Call out the foot and the type of pass to use.

(2.2) Passing Against a Wall

Purpose. To practice passes and passing accuracy.

Organization. Each player has a ball and passes or shoots against a rebound wall.

Directions. Call out the foot and type of pass. Players can select a spot or a target on the wall to hit. This drill can also be used as a skill check. Position players 15 to 30 ft from the wall and have them pass against it for 30 sec. Record players' scores and chart their progress throughout the season.

(2.3) Knocking Over Cones

Purpose. To develop passing accuracy.

Organization. Pair up players, with one ball per pair. Position each pair in a 10- by 10-yd grid with one cone or other target in the center.

Directions. Players stand along the edges or in the corners of the grid and pass the ball to hit the target. Help players to develop passing skills with both feet and develop specific passes by calling out which foot and the type of pass to use.

(2.4) Marbles

Purpose. To develop passing accuracy.

Organization. Pair up players and provide each player with a ball.

Directions. Marbles can be played by two or more players, but groups of two or three are best. One player begins by passing his or her ball a short distance. Other players then take turns passing to hit the ball. Each time a player hits the targeted ball, that player scores one point. Another player then kicks his or her ball, and the other players try to pass and hit the ball. If no player can hit the ball, the player who passed nearest scores a point. Play to 5 or 10 points.

(2.5) Passing Circle

Purpose. To practice passes and communication.

Organization. Divide players into groups of five or six; make the groups large enough to form a small circle about 10 yd across but small enough to keep them active. Provide one ball for each group.

Directions. Players pass the ball to each other across the circle. Instruct players to alternate feet and types of passes. To encourage communication, have players call out the name of the teammate to whom he or she will pass.

Variations:

Circle Pass and Run is designed to develop movement after passing. After two minutes of passing across the circle, have players follow their pass by running behind and taking the place of the teammate to whom they passed.

Circle Pass With Center Player is designed to teach players to pass the ball to different positions. One player in the center passes the ball to each player around the circle and then joins the circle as another player takes the center position (see Figure 2-14). Have players call out the name of the teammate to whom he or she will pass.

Fig. 2-14

(2.6) Passing on the Move

Purpose. To practice passing to a moving player.

Organization. Divide the group into pairs, with one ball per pair, within a 30- by 30-yd area.

Directions. Instruct players to move around within the playing area and to stay 10 to 15 yd away from each other. Encourage the passer to look for the receiver and the receiver to call for a pass.

Variations:

Passing to Corners is a fun game designed to develop a feel for passing accurately and to develop the proper timing for passes. The passer stands with a ball in a corner of a 10- by 10-yd grid while the receiver runs to one of the three open corners. The passer tries to pass so the ball arrives at the corner when the receiver does (see Figure 2-15). The receiver then becomes the passer, and the partner runs to an empty corner. Alternate feet and types of passes.

Fig. 2-15

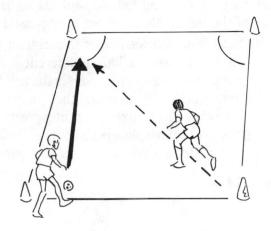

(2.7) Give-and-Go or Wall Passing 1

Purpose. To develop passing accuracy and to develop player movement to receive passes.

Organization. Divide your players into groups of three or four players and position them in lines facing each other about 15 yd apart, as shown in Figure 2-16. Provide one ball for every two groups.

Directions. The action of the ball should resemble passing to a wall and receiving the rebound. Player 1 passes to Player 2, who runs forward and to the side. Player 1 then runs directly ahead to receive a return pass from Player 2. Finally, Player 1 pushes the ball to Player 3, who begins this same sequence from the other side by passing to Player 4. Each passer and receiver moves to the end of a line when his or her turn is complete. Explain that this is an excellent passing tactic to move the ball around and between defenders during games.

Fig. 2-16

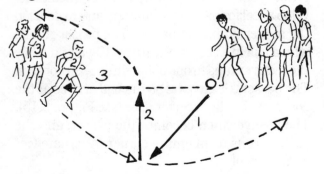

(2.8) Target Ball

Purpose. To develop chipping accuracy.

Organization. Mark a target of three zones using cones or other markers. As shown in Figure 2-17, the center zone is worth 20 points, the middle zone is worth 15 points, and the outside zone is worth 10 points. Pair up players, with one ball per pair. Position players on opposite sides of the target.

Directions. Each player stands 10 to 30 yd from the target, depending on the players' ages and abilities. Each player passes five times with each foot. After one player passes, the other player brings the ball under control and moves into position to pass. Vary the drill by specifying the foot and the type of pass. The player who scores the most points wins.

Fig. 2-17

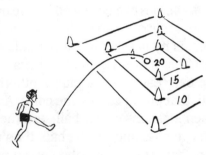

(2.9) Soccer Golf

Purpose. To develop accuracy for all types of passes.

Organization. Set out a series of cones as *holes* around the soccer field at varying distances to form a golf course as shown in Figure 2-18. Other holes can be trees, water fountains, telephone poles, or other convenient targets. Each player has a ball and can play alone or in groups of up to four players.

Directions. Every "hole" should require (a) a drive or long, lofted pass, (b) a chip or short, lofted pass, and (c) a putt or short pass along the ground. A ball is "sunk" when the cone or other target is hit. As in regular golf, the lowest score wins.

Fig. 2-18

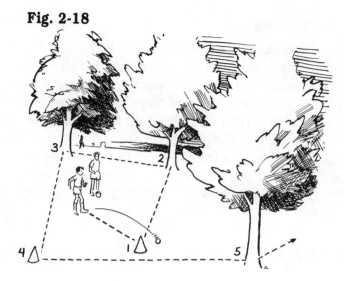

(2.10) Hunter

Purpose. To practice passing to moving targets.

Organization. Choose one player to be the hunter. This player stands in an area 15 by 30 yd with all the balls, while all other players (called "runners" or "animals") stand outside at one end of the area (see Figure 2-19).

Directions. Runners try to run from one end of the area to the other end without being hit below the knee by a pass from the hunter. You can increase the fun for more experienced players by specifying that passes be made with the outside or the instep of the foot only. Players hit with a ball become hunters and help to "shoot" other runners. The game continues until only one player remains. This last player becomes the hunter for the next game.

Fig. 2-19

(2.11) Call and Run

Purpose. To encourage communication, moving without the ball, and passing accuracy.

Organization. Divide the team into groups of five or six players and position them in a grid 20 by 20 yd or larger. Provide one ball per group.

Directions. One player begins with the ball and passes to another player, who runs toward the passer and calls for a pass. After passing the ball the passer moves to another area of the grid, and the receiver passes to another player who calls and runs toward the ball (see Figure 2-20).

Fig. 2-20

(2.12) Circle Keep-Away

Purpose. To develop awareness of opponents and passing accuracy.

Organization. Divide the team into groups of six to eight players, and have them form a circle about 10 yd in diameter with one player standing in the center (see Figure 2-21). Provide one ball per group.

Directions. Instruct the players around the circle to keep the ball away from the player in the center. The player in the center tries to steal the ball. If the ball is stolen or is passed out of the circle, the player in the center takes the place of the player who passed the ball.

Coaching Points. Tell your players to gain control and keep possession of the ball to attract the challenging or defending player before passing. This is called *committing the defender* and allows the next receiver more space and time to control and pass the ball. Also, this is how players should control and possess the ball in games.

Fig. 2-21

(2.13) Passing Long and High

Purpose. To develop long passing skill.

Organization. Pair up players, with one ball per pair. Position players at opposite ends of four 10- by 10-yd grids, as shown in Figure 2-22.

Directions. Instruct players to loft the ball 10 times with each foot from within their end of the playing area to their partners. Older, more experienced players can also practice curving the ball. The receiving player should try to control the ball within five or six yd.

Fig. 2-22

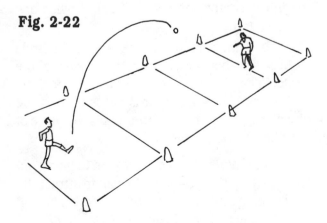

Variations:

Two Players in a Grid is designed to develop chip passing. Pair up players and position them in three 10- by 10-yd grids. The passer begins with the ball at one end and chips to the other end over the partner standing in the middle grid (see Figure 2-23). The partner then runs to collect the ball and repeats the procedure from the other far end as the partner now plays in the middle grid. Have players repeat this drill 10 times with each foot.

Fig. 2-23

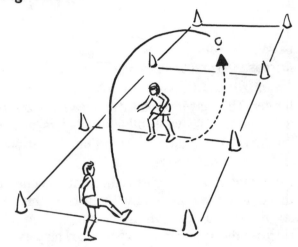

When players have developed sufficient chipping skill, add an additional player as a defender. This additional player stands in the center grid and can reach to block passes with the hands. Players switch positions after chipping five times with each foot.

Passing Long and High In Offense is designed to develop long passing skills under pressure from other players, as in an actual game. Choose teams of two offensive players and three defensive players or two versus two, plus one goalkeeper (see Figure 2-24). The offensive players attempt to loft passes over defenders to attack the goal. Passes should be made from in front and from either side of the goal.

Fig. 2-24

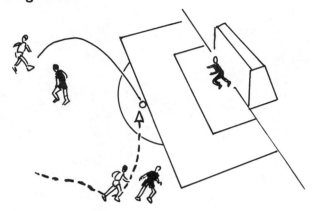

Four Versus Two is designed to develop chipping skills under pressure from other players. This game pits four offensive players against two defensive players in three 10- by 10-yd grids (see Figure 2-25). Two or three offensive players are positioned in one end of the playing area, and one offensive player is positioned in the other end. Defensive players cannot enter the grid that has only one player in it. The other two or three offensive players try to keep the ball away from the defenders and chip the ball to the offensive player at the far end. After each successful pass, additional offensive players must hustle down to initiate play from the other end of the grid. One hint for defenders is to position one defender in the middle grid to collect chip passes that fall short.

Fig. 2-25

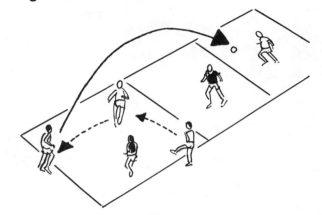

Chapter 3: Receiving and Controlling

Introduction: The Important First Touch

One way to describe a talented soccer player is as one who "always seems to have a lot of time." Good players appear to receive and control the ball so quickly that it seems a long time before that player is challenged by an opponent. This point reflects the importance of a player's first touch on the ball. The first touch can help determine how he or she controls the ball, passes to teammates, dribbles around opponents, or shoots at the goal. Less skilled players require more time and more touches to control and move the ball, giving their opponents more time to defend against them. Learning to receive and control the ball effectively requires considerable practice in specific receiving and controlling techniques. The following topics in this chapter are presented to help you teach receiving and controlling skills to your players:

- The Aim Is Ball Control
- Fundamentals of Receiving and Controlling
- Receiving Techniques
- Juggling
- Teaching Progression for Receiving and Controlling
- Games and Activities for Receiving and Controlling

The Aim Is Ball Control

Soccer can be thought of as a large game of keep-away using the feet. The better one team can control the ball and keep it away from the opposing players, the better chance that team will have to score and to win the game. Thus, ball control is an important objective of good team play. Explain to your players that, in order to control balls passed to them, they must *keep the ball close to the feet*. Near the feet, the ball is easier to pass, dribble, or shoot, but if the ball gets beyond a player it is easier for opponents to steal.

Fundamentals of Receiving and Controlling

Because most young people grow up learning to catch with their hands, this method of receiving and controlling a ball is relatively easy. This is especially true in baseball and softball, where players use gloves to help them catch and control. In soccer, however, players cannot use the arms or hands (see Figure 3-1), but must use the feet, legs, or body to receive the ball. Controlling the ball once it is received is also difficult because the feet cannot hold the ball the way the hands can. Thus, specific techniques must be used to receive and to control passes.

As in catching with the hands, a player tends to use his or her dominant foot or leg to receive passes. Encourage players to learn to receive passes equally well with one foot or the other. Two drills that will help your players learn these fundamentals are Toss and Receive (3.1) and Quick Control (3.2).

Fig. 3-1

Each technique involves the body part used to receive the pass and whether the ball is slowed, or *cushioned*, or whether it is trapped quickly against the ground, or *wedged*.

Regardless of the technique used, four fundamental components or stages are common to receive and control passes: (a) *move in line with the ball*, (b) *reach out to meet the ball*, (c) *cushion or wedge the ball* with the appropriate foot surface, and (d) *control the ball with the feet*. To help you teach players receiving and controlling techniques, each component is discussed separately. We recognize, however, that these divisions do not naturally occur on the playing field, and we recommend you present these four components as progressive stages within each receiving technique (see Figures 3-2 to 3-5).

Move in Line With the Ball

To be in position to receive the ball with the feet, legs, or body, your players must learn to judge the distance, speed, and direction of the ball, and then to move in line with or in front of the ball (see Figure 3-2). But learning to judge a rolling or bouncing ball is not easy for young players.

Help your players develop this skill by progressing in the following manner. First, for young and inexperienced players, roll and toss the ball to them so they can control it. Second, for players with more experience, roll and toss the ball while players run to move in line with the ball. Third, for players with even more experience, develop practices that simulate game situations and encourage players to move in line with the ball.

Fig. 3-2

Reach Out to Meet the Ball

As the ball approaches your players, they will need to decide which part of the body should receive the ball. Your players can receive the ball with any part of the body, except the hands and arms. The important point is to maintain balance and to reach out to meet the ball. To demonstrate, follow the example shown in Figure 3-3. Point out that, although they may need to stand on one foot and reach with the other foot, they must maintain their balance and stay in line with the ball.

Fig. 3-3

Cushion or Wedge the Ball

To receive the ball, the player should relax the body part receiving the ball and withdraw or move it in the same direction as the ball (see Figure 3-4). Explain that cushioning the ball will help players control it and keep it close to their feet. To help your players understand how important this is, have them stop fairly quick passes from you with a stiff leg. Point out how difficult it is to control the ball and how far the ball rolls away. Then have them cushion the ball and notice the difference.

Fig. 3-4

Another method used to control the ball is to wedge the ball between the foot and the ground. This is very effective for receiving a ball falling from the air (see Figure 3-5). This is an advanced skill, however, and should be introduced to players who are well skilled and who are proficient at receiving passes on the ground.

Fig. 3-5

Control the Ball With the Feet

After receiving the ball, your players should keep it close to their feet so they can pass or dribble quickly. This sounds easy, but it really is difficult. Not every ball will stop in front of the feet, therefore your players should be ready to move around and retrieve a ball that rolls away. They should never stand flat footed!

Coaching Points for the Fundamentals of Receiving and Controlling

1. Do not stand still. Move to the ball and in line with the ball.
2. Receive the ball by reaching out to meet the ball and cushioning or wedging the ball to a stop. Be sure to maintain balance.
3. Advanced players can receive the ball by wedging it against the ground.
4. Follow the ball and control it with the feet.
5. Practice receiving with the left foot as well as with the right foot.

Receiving Techniques

Any part of the body, except the hands, can be used to receive and control the ball. The body parts that are most mobile and can best manipulate the ball are the *inside, outside, instep,* and *sole of the foot,* the *thigh,* and the *chest.* Explain to your players that the technique they choose to receive the ball should be determined by whether the ball is on the ground or in the air. The inside, outside, and sole of the foot can be used to receive passes on the ground. The inside and outside of the foot, instep, thigh, and chest are commonly used to receive passes in the air.

Passes on the ground are easier to receive than passes in the air, and until players can execute long, lofted passes proficiently, receiving passes on the ground will be the most common method used in games. Thus, we recommend that you teach players the techniques for receiving passes on the ground first. Then, when they can use long, lofted passes in games, teach the techniques for receiving passes in the air.

Receiving Passes on the Ground

The inside, outside, and sole of the foot are most often used to receive passes on the ground, but the method used to receive the ball with the inside and outside of the foot is different from that used for receiving with the sole of the foot. Demonstrate that because the player can withdraw the leg and allow the side of the foot to slow the ball, the player can use the inside and outside of the foot to cushion the ball (see Figure 3-6). Because the sole of the foot can be raised and lowered easily, it is used to wedge the ball against the ground.

Fig. 3-6

Inside and Outside of Foot

Explain that receiving passes on the ground is the reverse of passing to teammates. As the ball approaches, players move in line with the ball, reach out to meet the ball, cushion the ball, and control it with the feet. Because the inside of the foot has a larger surface area to control the ball than the outside of the foot, receiving passes with the inside of the foot is a bit easier than with the outside of the foot.

Sole of the Foot

Wedging the ball against the ground is not as easy as it seems. The foot must be raised so that the heel is slightly off the ground and the toes are pointed up (see Figure 3-7). Then, as the ball rolls under the foot, the toes are lowered, and the ball is trapped. A coaching hint for this technique is to keep the ankle and knee relaxed to absorb the force of the ball. If the foot is raised very far off the ground, the ball will roll underneath. Also, if the foot is held too stiffly or lands on the ball too hard, the ball will bounce away from the foot.

Fig. 3-7

Coaching Points for Receiving Passes on the Ground

1. Cushioning passes is the reverse of kicking passes; reach out to the ball, cushion it, and control it.
2. Wedge the ball by raising the foot—keeping the heel low and pointing the toes—and then lowering the foot on top of the ball.
3. Practice with the left foot as well as with the right foot.
4. Do not wedge the ball hard, or the ball will bounce away.

Receiving Passes From the Air

Receiving passes from the air is more difficult than receiving passes on the ground. Players must judge the height of the ball as well as either cushion the ball falling from the air to the ground (see Figure 3-8), or wedge the ball between the foot and the ground (see Figure 3-9). Both methods require precise timing. The body parts used to cushion passes are the instep, thigh, and chest. The sole, inside, and outside of the foot are used to wedge passes. The Wedge Direction Drill (3.3) is a fun drill that will help your players learn to receive and direct passes from the air.

Fig. 3-8

Fig. 3-9

Instep and Thigh

Because the surface area of the instep and the thigh is large, these may be your players' body parts best used for receiving passes from the air. Also, the softness of the thigh helps cushion the ball. These two methods are similar to receiving passes on the ground with the inside and outside of the foot. Demonstrate how to raise the body part to meet the ball and to relax or withdraw the body part to cushion the ball, as shown in Figure 3-10. Also encourage your players to drop the ball close to their feet and to be ready to move with the ball if it rolls away.

Fig. 3-10

Chest

We recommend that you teach all players to trap with the chest. Progress from easy tosses for younger players, to throw-ins, chips, and long passes for older players. Encourage your players to learn this skill and to use it in games as they feel comfortable and demonstrate their ability to use it effectively.

To receive with the chest, your players should stand in front of the ball, push out the chest, then relax or pull the chest back as the ball makes contact, dropping the ball in front and near the feet. Follow the ball to control it with the feet (see Figure 3-11 to 3-13). Players can maintain balance and stability by spreading the legs about shoulder width apart to form a strong base of support.

Fig. 3-11

Fig. 3-12

Fig. 3-13

Sole of Foot

The most crucial component of wedging passes from the air with the sole of the foot is timing, because the ball must be wedged just as it hits the ground. As shown above in Figure 3-14, show your players how to point the toes to angle the foot and how to place the foot on top of the ball as it contacts the ground. Again, keeping the ankle and the knee relaxed will help absorb the impact of the ball. Practice this with short, easy tosses and gradually progress to long passes.

Fig. 3-14

Inside and Outside of Foot

The purposes of receiving passes from the air with the inside and outside of the foot are to control the ball with one touch and to guide the ball in a particular direction with the same touch. Young, beginning players may need to use one touch to receive the ball and another to pass. As players mature and gain experience they will develop the ability to receive and direct the ball with one touch. Directing the ball can be used to pass to teammates or to begin a dribble. To do this your players will need to wedge the ball and direct it in the desired direction (see Figure 3-15). An important hint that will help to stop the ball near the feet is to keep the ankle and leg relaxed rather than stiff.

Fig. 3-15

Coaching Points for Receiving Passes From the Air

1. Cushion easy passes with the instep and thigh.
2. Watch the pass all the way to the ground.
3. Control high passes by cushioning with the chest.
4. Wedge fast, low passes with the sole of the foot. Do not wedge too hard or the ball will bounce away.
5. Use a first touch to stop the ball and a second touch to direct the ball. As players gain experience they can receive and direct the ball with one touch.
6. Practice with the left foot as well as with the right foot.

Juggling

Juggling, or keeping the ball in the air, is a particularly useful skill to develop good ball control, and you should encourage your players to juggle regularly. Also, it is one of the soccer skills that players can practice by themselves in a limited area. Although players rarely juggle in actual games, the ball control developed by juggling helps players dribble, pass, receive, and control the ball. In fact, players who juggle well also tend to be players who control the ball well. Players can juggle with the feet, legs, and head;

they can use any part of the body except the arms and hands. But the most common ways to juggle are with the instep, thigh, and head. Two effective drills to develop juggling and ball control are Juggle Around the Circle (3.4) and Pepper (3.5).

As shown in Figures 3-16 to 3-18, a good method to introduce juggling is to have your players hold the ball, drop it onto the foot or thigh, softly kick it, and catch it. To juggle with the head, toss the ball, head it, and catch it. As your players become more proficient they should try to kick or head the ball twice and catch it, then three times and catch it. Eventually they will be able to juggle several times before losing control of the ball.

Fig. 3-16

Fig. 3-17

Fig. 3-18

Demonstrate that to juggle well (a) the foot, thigh, or head should make contact directly underneath the ball, (b) the foot, thigh, and head should be held horizontal or flat to the ball, not angled, (c) the eyes should watch the ball at all times, (d) the player should relax and not become overly tense, and (e) when heading, the legs should push the body and the head up and into the ball.

Teaching Progression for Receiving and Controlling

1. Teach players to keep the ball close to the feet.
2. Teach players the fundamentals of (a) moving in line with the ball, (b) reaching out to meet the ball, (c) cushioning or wedging the ball, (d) controlling the ball with the feet.
3. Teach players the techniques for receiving passes on the ground with the inside, outside, and sole of the foot. Practice with the left foot as well as with the right foot.
4. Teach players to receive the ball with one touch and to direct the ball with a second touch. Gradually progress to receiving and directing the ball with one touch.
5. Teach more able players the techniques for receiving passes from the air with the thigh and the chest.
6. Teach more able players the techniques for wedging and directing passes from the air with the sole, inside, and outside of the foot.

Games and Activities for Receiving and Controlling

(3.1) Toss and Receive

Purpose. To practice receiving and controlling passes.

Organization. Players pair up, with one ball per pair. Players stand apart far enough to toss and receive the ball.

Directions. Practice receiving and controlling techniques appropriate for the players' age level. Practice receiving with the left foot as well as with the right foot. As a skill-check variation, have the receiver try to control the ball within two steps of his or her position. Score one point if the ball is kept within two steps. Subtract one point if the player cannot. Try 10 with each foot and 10 with the chest.

(3.2) Quick Control

Purpose. To practice receiving fundamentals.

Organization. Divide players into groups of two, with two balls per group. Players stand about 5 yd apart.

Directions. One player tosses balls to his or her teammate in rapid succession while the receiver controls the ball and passes it back. Switch roles after 10 passes. Another way to practice receiving is to have players form a circle, with one player standing in the center receiving and returning balls tossed by teammates. Switch after a player completes two revolutions.

(3.3) Wedge Direction

Purpose. To practice wedge control.

Organization. Divide players into groups of three, with one ball per group. Players stand about 5 to 10 yd apart and form a triangle.

Directions. Players practice tossing balls in the air to each other and receiving with wedge control, then practice passing balls to the next player (see Figure 3-19). Players should use one touch to wedge the ball and another touch to pass the ball. Toss and control clockwise and counterclockwise.

Fig. 3-19

(3.4) Juggle Around the Circle

Purpose. To develop receiving and ball control skills.

Organization. Divide players into groups of five or six players. Have the groups form circles, with one ball per group.

Directions. Players try to juggle the ball around or across the circle. Count the number of times the ball is juggled. Another variation is to call out the name of a player and juggle to that player, who calls out and passes to another player. Also, a player can be placed in the center and juggle to each player in sequence. Switch players in the center after each revolution.

(3.5) Pepper

Purpose. To practice ball control skills.

Organization. Divide players into groups of four to six, with one ball per group. One player is the kicker and the remaining players spread out from left (end of line) to right (front of line) 5 to 10 yd in front of the kicker.

Directions. The kicker passes the ball on the ground or in the air and the receiver must return the ball in the same manner. If the kicker miskicks, he or she moves to the end of the line and the player at the front of the line becomes the kicker. If the receiver cannot control the ball or miskicks, he or she moves to the end of the line (see Figure 3-20).

Fig. 3-20

(3.6) Receive and Control Under Pressure

Purpose. To develop the ability to receive the ball and to control it while being challenged by a defender.

Organization. Pair up players and position them in a 10- by 10-yd grid, with one ball per pair.

Directions. One player is the receiver, and one player is the passer/defender. Position the receiver about 3 yd in from the side of the grid. The passer/defender is positioned on the opposite side of the grid. The passer passes to the receiver and runs toward him or her to challenge for the ball. The receiver receives the ball and tries to dribble to one of the two nearest cones behind him or her (see Figure 3-21). Rotate positions after every five passes. You can make this game more difficult by requiring the receiver to dribble or pass the ball to one of the two farthest cones in front of him or her.

Fig. 3-21

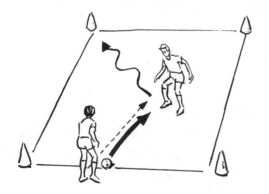

Variations:

Receiving and Turning in Threes is designed to develop the ability to receive passes and to turn with the ball while being challenged. Divide players into groups of three and position them in a 10- by 10-yd grid, with one ball per group. Position one player in the center of the grid and the other two players along opposite sides (see Figure 3-22) of the grid. One player on the side passes the ball to the player in the center, who receives the ball and turns to pass to the other teammate. Players rotate positions after every five passes.

Fig. 3-22

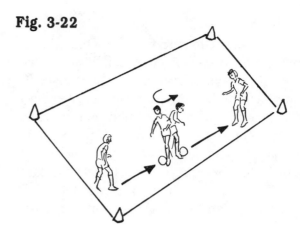

(3.7) Control, Pass, and Follow Pass

Purpose. To develop ball control and one-touch passing.

Organization. Divide your team into four equal lines of at least two but not more than four players and position them about 10 yd apart facing a central position (see Figure 3-23), with one ball per four groups.

Directions. The player with the ball passes it to the front of another line and joins the back of that line. The player that receives the ball can pass the ball to the front of another line. You can specify the surface of the foot players must use to receive and pass the ball. The ultimate objective of this drill is to develop the ability to receive, control, and pass, touching the ball only once. Young, inexperienced players should begin by using one touch to receive and control the ball and a second touch to pass the ball. As you notice your players improving in their skills, encourage them to receive and pass with one touch.

Fig. 3-23

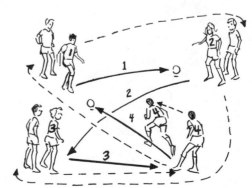

Variations:

Scramble is a one-touch passing drill played with three or more players and one ball. Position two players (the player in front has the ball) about 10 yd across from the third player. The player with the ball passes to the third player, then runs around behind this player. The player who received the pass now passes with one touch of the ball to the next player, then follows the pass (see Figure 3-24). Continue this cycle for 3 to 5 minutes. Caution players about running too fast and speeding up the game. A consistent, steady pace is better than a fast, ragged pace.

Fig. 3-24

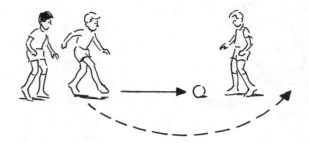

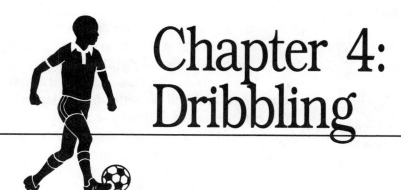

Chapter 4: Dribbling

Introduction: Individual Ball Control

The ability to control and keep possession of the ball against opponents is a very important soccer skill. Often your players must dribble around opponents in order to pass or shoot. The challenge between an individual dribbling against a defender is exciting and often results in spectacular plays—even for young players. Another situation where a player finds dribbling skill valuable is in a fast break, where a player advances the ball in the open field when no defenders are around and teammates are not yet in position to receive passes. The following topics are present in this chapter to help you teach dribbling to your players:

- Dribbling Fundamentals
- Dribbling Techniques
- Faking to Beat Opponents
- Teaching Progression for Dribbling
- Games and Activities for Dribbling

Dribbling Fundamentals

Your young soccer players may think dribbling is simply kicking the ball and chasing after it. But they must learn that dribbling means being able to control the ball and move it in various directions by (a) using the inside and outside of the feet, (b) using both the right foot and the left foot, and (c) using small steps and light touches.

Three common errors that young players face in learning to dribble are looking down at the ball rather than up at opponents and teammates, losing the ball by always dribbling with the inside of the same foot, and dribbling faster than they can control the ball. These errors can be corrected by teaching your players (a) to dribble with the inside and outside of the feet, (b) to look up when dribbling, (c) to dribble with the right foot and left foot, (d) to dribble with small steps and light touches, and (e) to develop control first and speed later or dribble only as fast as you can control the ball.

Several drills have been designed to help your player practice and develop these skills. The Dribble Around Cones Drill (4.1) will help players dribble with several light touches and move the ball in a zigzag pattern. Bee Hive (4.2) is a fun game designed to help players develop a feel for the ball and, with the How Many Fingers Drill (4.3), will help players remember to look up when dribbling. The Relay Races Drill (4.4) is a fun game that tests players' ability to dribble fast while maintaining control of the ball.

Dribble With the Inside and Outside of the Feet

Effective players are able to adapt to different situations in games, because they can manipulate the ball with any surface of the foot. Demonstrate how to *direct the ball with the inside and outside of the feet*. To dribble with the inside of the foot, turn the foot out. To dribble with the outside of the foot, turn the foot in.

37

Dribble With the Right Foot and the Left Foot

Although players can change direction using the inside and outside of the foot, their effectiveness will be limited if they dribble with only one foot. Just as basketball players should learn to dribble well with each hand, soccer players should learn to dribble well with each foot. This is important because many players are predictable when dribbling if they dribble exclusively with their preferred foot. This makes the task of the defensive players easier because they can anticipate the moves of the dribbler. The ability to dribble with the nondominant foot requires much practice and may take several years to fully develop. Therefore, the sooner young players begin practicing, the sooner this will develop.

Dribble With Small Steps and Light Touches

Encourage players to move with short steps and many, light touches rather than by kicking the ball long distances ahead of the body. This will help your players keep the ball close to their feet, change direction quickly and easily, and dribble around opponents when space is limited.

Dribble Looking Up

Players who dribble while constantly looking at the ball tend to dribble too much, fail to see teammates to whom they can pass, and fail to see opponents guarding them. This makes players ineffective, because their attention is not focused on the action around them. Demonstrate how to dribble by feel with the head up, occasionally looking at the ball when necessary (see Figure 4-1). To teach this, have your players begin by dribbling at a walk while looking around. Gradually progress to dribbling at a jog, and finally at a running pace.

Dribble Only as Fast as You Can Control the Ball

Players with good speed do not automatically have *quick feet*, and the faster players run, the less control they have to stop, change direction, pass, or shoot. Therefore, encourage your players to dribble only as fast as they can control the ball. If players follow this dribbling fundamental they will be less likely to lose possession of the ball to opponents and will be better team players.

You can demonstrate this to your players by having them dribble up to and around two cones spaced 10 yd apart; first at a jog, second, a bit faster, and third, as fast as possible. Each time they dribble faster, moving around the cone becomes more difficult. Specific dribbling techniques to slow, stop, and change direction of the ball are discussed in the next section.

Fig. 4-1

Coaching Points for Dribbling Fundamentals

1. Dribble with the inside and outside of the feet.
2. Dribble with the right foot and the left foot.
3. Dribble with small steps and light touches.
4. Dribble looking up for teammates and defenders.
5. Dribble only as fast as you can control the ball.

Dribbling Techniques

After your players have learned to dribble reasonably well following the dribbling fundamentals, they will be ready to learn specific techniques for *running with the ball* and for *stopping and changing direction*. While running with the ball is fairly straightforward and is used to quickly advance the ball over long distances, changing direction is more complicated and uses several foot surfaces to maneuver the ball. Quick changes of direction are quite effective in deceiving opponents and avoiding defensive players. Players who are not necessarily fast can still be effective if they can change direction quickly in crowded areas.

Running With the Ball

The main objective of dribbling in the open field is either to move the ball into open space away from opponents or to quickly advance to the opponents' goal, before the defense can mark players and guard against the attack. If opponents are not in the way, close ball control is not so important. Consequently, the ball can be played further in front of the body, and players can actually *run with the ball* (see Figure 4-2). Explain that to run with the ball, players should follow the fundamentals of dribbling as fast as they can while both controlling the ball and looking up to see teammates and defenders.

Fig. 4-2

Stopping and Changing Direction

Because running with the ball does not require great ball control or foot coordination, even relatively inexperienced players can learn this quickly. Much more difficult, however, is stopping the ball and changing its direction. These moves require good ball control and coordination with *the sole, inside, and outside of the foot.*

Players will learn best if taught in a purposeful progression. First have them stop and change the direction of the ball while walking. Gradually progress to having them perform these tasks while jogging, then while running. Again, encourage players to use their right feet as well as their left feet. Red Light, Green Light (4.5), Stop and Go Drill (4.6), Obstacle Course (4.7), and the Shuttle Run Skill Check (4.8) are excellent activities to practice stopping and changing direction of the ball.

Sole of the Foot

The sole of the foot is used to stop the ball and change its direction quickly, as shown in Figure 4-3. Demonstrate how to balance on one foot and gently touch the top of the ball with the sole of the other foot. From this position, the ball can be rolled forward, backward, or to either side by moving the foot.

Although stopping the ball with the sole of the foot is relatively easy, stopping the ball and changing its direction is more difficult. To teach your players to turn 180 degrees and then move forward, tell your players to drag the ball back with the sole of the foot, let it roll behind them, and dribble away. To teach them to turn 90 degrees, have your players drag the ball back and push it away at a 90-degree angle with the inside of the same foot.

Fig. 4-3

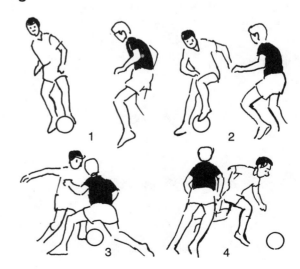

Inside and Outside of the Foot

Turning the ball with the inside and outside of the foot is an effective way for players to change the ball's direction without stopping completely. Turning with the inside of the foot (Figure 4-4) begins by swinging the foot around the ball to hook it, pivoting on the other foot in the desired direction, and pulling the ball. The right foot is used to move to the left and the left foot is used to move to the right.

Fig. 4-4

Turning with the outside of the foot is similar, but a bit more difficult because players tend to turn away from the pivot foot rather than toward the pivot foot (see Figure 4-5). Show them how to swing the foot around the ball, hook it with the outside of the foot, and turn it in the desired direction. Explain that the right foot is used to move to the right and the left foot is used to move to the left.

Fig. 4-5

Shielding the Ball

When a player has possession of the ball but has no passing options and is under pressure from an opponent, the ball must be protected or *shielded*. To shield the ball, players should place their body between the ball and the defender, controlling the ball with all surfaces of the foot (see Figure 4-6). In this side position, the dribbler can see the opponent, keep the ball away from the opponent, and prevent the opponent from reaching through the legs to kick the ball.

Fig. 4-6

Coaching Points for Dribbling Techniques

1. When in the open field and unguarded, run with the ball. Because the danger of losing possession of the ball is not great in this situation, a player can push the ball farther from the body than he or she would when more closely guarded.
2. Stop the dribble and change the direction of the ball by touching the top of it with the sole of the foot and pushing or dragging the ball in the direction desired.
3. Change the direction of the ball with the inside or the outside of the foot by hooking the foot around it, pivoting on the other foot, and pushing the ball in the direction desired.
4. Shield the ball, when guarded closely and unable to pass, by turning the side of the body to the opponent and controlling the ball with all surfaces of the foot.

Faking to Beat Opponents

Pretending to move in one direction and actually moving in another, or *faking*, is an advanced part of dribbling used to fool defenders. Because fakes are complicated skills, we suggest you teach them only to players, regardless of age, who have good dribbling fundamentals. Some players under 10 years will be skilled enough to learn fakes; some players over 10 years will not.

Many dribbling fakes have been developed by soccer players and some of your players may develop their own moves to beat opponents. The most common fakes are *side-step fakes, step-over fakes,* and *pass fakes.*

Side-Step Fakes

When a player appears to be preparing to dribble in one direction, then dribbles in the opposite one, he or she is using a side-step fake (see Figures 4-7 and 4-8). To fake left and dribble right, demonstrate how to (a) step quickly with the left foot to the left of the ball, (b) swing the right foot along the left side of the ball, as if to move left, and (c) push the ball to the right with the outside of the right foot. To fake right and move left, simply alternate feet on the right side of the ball. Pushing the head, shoulders, and arms to the side of the fake can really help fool opponents.

Fig. 4-7

Fig. 4-8

Step-Over Fakes

Step-over fakes are more complicated than side-step fakes and are used to move from side to side (see Figure 4-9) and to reverse direction (see Figure 4-10). This is accomplished by stepping over the ball in one direction and tapping the ball in the opposite direction. Because the footwork is complicated, it is a good idea to demonstrate and practice this fake slowly, gradually moving faster as your players develop their moves.

Fig. 4-9

Fig. 4-10

Demonstrate how to fake and move right by (a) placing the right foot to the right side and behind the ball, (b) swinging the left foot over the ball, as if to dribble forward, (c) swinging the left foot to the left side of the ball, and (d) swinging the right foot to the left side of the ball and push to the right. To fake and move to the left, alternate feet and execute on the left side of the ball.

Demonstrate how to step over and reverse direction by (a) stepping over the ball with the right foot, (b) placing the left foot beside the right foot, and (c) pushing the ball in the opposite direction with the outside of the right foot and dribbling away.

Pass Fakes

Players can fake from a pass by playing the ball in front of the body or by playing the ball behind the body. The initial motion for each method is to plant the nonkicking foot near the ball and to swing the kicking foot toward the ball as if to pass it, step over the ball, and reverse the direction or dribble away.

To play the ball behind the body, pretend to pass but drag the ball with the inside of the foot behind the nonkicking foot. This is a difficult skill even for many proficient dribblers, so you should wait until your players demonstrate that they are effective dribblers before teaching them this skill. One hint that will make this skill a bit easier is to place the nonkicking foot ahead of the ball. The defensive player usually will not notice this and the nonkicking foot will not block the ball.

Coaching Points for Faking to Beat Opponents

1. Fake to one side, as if to dribble in that direction, then push the ball in the opposite direction.
2. Fake by stepping over the ball, as if to continue dribbling, then push the ball to one side, or reverse the direction.
3. Fake by pretending to pass the ball, then push it to one side in front of or behind the body.

4. Use the head, shoulders, and arms to make the fake appear realistic.

Teaching Progression for Dribbling

1. Teach players to use the inside and outside of the feet.
2. Teach players to dribble with each foot.
3. Teach players to dribble using small steps and light touches.
4. Teach players to dribble with the head up.
5. Teach players to dribble only as fast as they can control the ball.
6. Teach players to run with the ball.
7. Teach players to stop and change the direction of the ball with the sole, inside, and outside of foot.
8. Teach players side fakes, step-over fakes, and pass fakes.

Games and Activities for Dribbling

In addition to the dribbling activities specified in this chapter to help players develop their individual dribbling skills, your players will need to practice dribbling against opponents in game situations. King of the Ring (4.9), Tag (4.10), Rats and Rabbits (4.11), and Combat Zone (4.12) are fun games designed to help players learn to dribble around opponents in confined areas and to protect the ball.

(4.1) Dribble Around Cones

Purpose. To practice dribbling with several light touches in a zigzag pattern.

Organization. Place six cones or other markers in a line about 6 ft apart. Have players form several lines so several can dribble at the same time. Each player has a ball.

Directions. Players dribble in and out of each cone, around the last cone, and back to the start. You can time how long players take to dribble back and forth. As the season progresses, their times should decrease.

(4.2) Bee Hive

Purpose. To practice ball control using several light touches.

Organization. Use cones or other objects to mark a 15–20-yd area. Each player has a ball, and each player dribbles at the same time.

Directions. Players dribble through the area trying not to touch other players or lose their control of the balls.

(4.3) How Many Fingers?

Purpose. To practice dribbling by "feel," without looking at the ball.

Organization. Divide players into groups of five or six; each player has a ball. Each group forms a large circle around the coach or player in the center.

Directions. Players dribble around the coach, who holds up his or her hand showing a certain number of fingers for three seconds. The coach then drops the hand. Players are asked to shout the number of fingers shown.

(4.4) Relay Races

Purpose. To practice dribbling and reversing the ball's direction.

Organization. Divide players into equal teams of at least three players each, with one ball for each team. Determine a starting line and a turn-around line.

Directions. One player from each team races up and back, passing to the next player who begins after the previous dribbler crosses the starting line. Players sit down after they have dribbled. The first team to have all players finish the course wins. Teams are disqualified if a player kicks the ball and runs rather than dribbling, or if a player begins his or her turn before the previous dribbler crosses the starting line.

(4.5) Red Light, Green Light

Purpose. To practice dribbling and stopping.

Organization. Designate one player as the "caller"; all other players are dribblers. The caller stands at one sideline with his or her back to the dribblers, who stand at the other sideline.

Directions. Dribblers dribble toward the caller when he or she shouts "Green light." They must stop and freeze when he or she shouts "Red light" and turns around. Players caught moving must return to the start. The first player to dribble beyond the caller wins and is the caller for the next game.

(4.6) Stop and Go

Purpose. To practice dribbling, stopping, and changing direction.

Organization. Each player has a ball and stands along a sideline. Coaches stand behind players.

Directions. Players dribble and follow the coach's instructions to "go" (dribble forward), "stop," or "reverse" direction.

(4.7) Obstacle Course

Purpose. To practice dribbling and changing direction freely.

Organization. Establish an obstacle course of cones, trees, balls, shoes, or other markers. Each player has a ball.

Directions. Players dribble around the course freely, moving in and around the cones or other markers.

(4.8) Shuttle Run Skill Check

Purpose. To practice and check your players' ability to dribble and reverse the ball's direction.

Organization. Mark two lines on the field, 10 yd apart (see Figure 4-11). Each player has a ball.

Directions. Players dribble one at a time, starting at one line and going back and forth until they have touched each line twice. You can time how long this takes and chart your players' progress throughout the season. As players become better dribblers, times will decrease.

Fig. 4-11

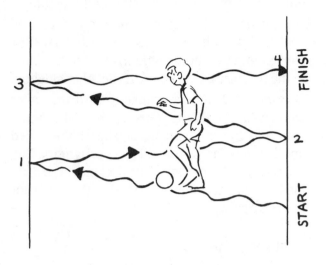

(4.9) King of the Ring

Purpose. To practice dribbling around other players using several light touches and protecting the ball.

Organization. Use cones or other objects to mark an area 15 to 20 yd square. Each player has a ball and dribbles inside this area.

Directions. Each player tries to kick any other player's ball out of the area while maintaining possession of his or her own ball. One point is scored for each ball kicked out of the area. Players whose balls are kicked out can return but must begin with zero points. The player with the most points is the winner. Suggested time is between one and two minutes per game.

(4.10) Tag

Purpose. To practice dribbling and changing direction.

Organization. Use cones or other objects to mark an area 15 to 20 yd square. Each player has a ball and dribbles inside this area.

Directions. This game has two variations. Variation One: Every player except one has a ball and dribbles in the area. The player without a ball is the "chaser" or "it" and tries to tag as many players as possible. Players who are tagged are frozen and must stand holding the ball over their heads with their feet spread apart. Frozen players can be "unfrozen" by other players dribbling balls through the frozen player's legs. Suggested time is one to two minutes per game. You can select two chasers if the game drags on.

Variation Two: Same as above except, as players are tagged, they join the chaser to tag other players. The game is over when only one player remains dribbling.

(4.11) Rats and Rabbits

Purpose. To practice reversing direction and dribbling away from opponents.

Organization. Divide the team into two equal groups and position them facing each other about 6 yd apart. One group is called "Rats"; the other is called "Rabbits." Use cones or other objects to mark a safety line 10 yd behind each group. Each player has a ball.

Directions. When you shout "Rats," the rats leave their balls and chase after the rabbits who must turn and dribble beyond the safety line. Roles are reversed when you shout "Rabbits." Teams score a point for each member of the other team tagged. However, if you shout a word that sounds like either rat or rabbit, such as "Rhubarb," each team gets a point for every player on the opposite team who moves. The team with the most points after three tries is the winner.

(4.12) Combat Zone

Purpose. To practice dribbling around opponents and protecting the ball.

Organization. Use cones or other objects to mark four 10- by 10-yd zones. Divide the team into two equal groups, an offensive group and a defensive group; each player in the offensive group has a ball (see Figure 4-12).

Directions. Defensive players can play only within the two combat zones (shaded). The offensive players dribble through the defensive or combat zones (shaded) into the other neutral zone. Defensive players try to tackle and kick the balls out of the area. A point is awarded for each player who successfully dribbles through the combat zones. Give each team three attempts, then reverse roles.

Fig. 4-12

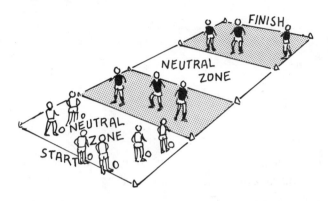

(4.13) Shadowchaser

Purpose. To practice faking and changing direction.

Organization. Pair up players, with one ball per pair. One player dribbles while the other tries to follow the ball. Place two cones about 5 yd apart as the playing area.

Directions. The dribbler stands on one side of an imaginary line between the two cones, while the *shadowchaser* stands on the other side of the imaginary line. The dribbler tries to fake and dribble to one cone, beating the shadowchaser who tries to keep up with the ball. The shadowchaser does not try to tackle or win the ball. Alternate roles after every five tries. Players keep track of the number of times they beat the shadowchaser to a cone.

(4.14) Running the Gauntlet

Purpose. To practice dribbling around opponents.

Organization. Use cones to mark four 10- by 10-yd grids. The cones at the back of the fourth grid mark the goal. Position one defender in each of the grids. The defender in the fourth grid serves as the goalkeeper. Offensive players should form a line at the top of the playing area, with one ball per player.

Directions. Each player attempts to dribble around the defenders and shoot for the goal. Other players in line should not enter the playing area until the previous player has shot for goal and the defenders are ready to begin. Players will rotate positions in the following manner: the shooter becomes the goalkeeper; the goalkeeper retrieves the ball and dribbles back to the end of the line; defenders become offensive players when they successfully take the ball away from the offense or you signal a change in position.

- As your players demonstrate the ability to dribble effectively, you can add defensive players who can move two steps in either direction to stop the ball (see Figure 4-13).

- For advanced players, defenders can move anywhere within the grid in which they are positioned.

Fig. 4-13

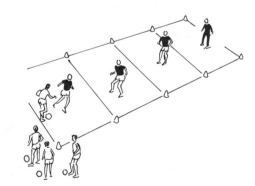

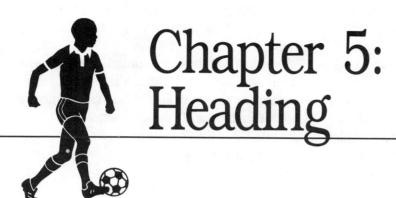

Chapter 5: Heading

Introduction: Heading Is Unique to Soccer

Heading is a technique unique to the sport of soccer, because no other sport uses the head to project the ball. Heading is used in a variety of situations: to pass, receive, and control the ball; to score; and to defend. A player can head the ball in any direction. Heading in each direction—forward, backward, or sideways—requires a slightly different technique.

Some young players may be apprehensive about heading because they fear getting hurt. As a coach, your challenge will be to teach your players to overcome the natural inclination to close the eyes as the ball approaches the head and the learned reaction to duck the head and turn away from the ball. One way to reduce this fear is to use balls that are soft and resilient, perhaps even letting the air out of some balls. For very young players, sponge rubber balls or light, rubber balls can be used. In fact, young players usually enjoy heading soft balls and, as they gain confidence, the transition to a soccer ball is quite easy.

Remember, the very first experience can leave lasting memories, so be sure the first few heading practices are fun and nonthreatening. A fun and effective first heading drill is Discover the Heading Surface (5.1). Also, develop heading skills in a sound, progressive manner, as outlined in this chapter. The following topics are presented in this chapter to help you teach heading to your players:

- Considering Your Players
- Heading Fundamentals and Teaching Progression
- Heading Forward
- Heading Sideways
- Heading Backward
- Heading in the Air
- Teaching Progression for Heading
- Games and Activities for Heading

Considering Your Players

Heading is not a skill that can be learned and used in a few short practice sessions. Instead, heading involves many components that your players may not directly understand but that are essential to effective soccer play. As a coach working with young soccer players, you must inform them of these components, not only for safety, but for future skill development. Heading is a skill that requires a certain degree of body control and strength to learn and use effectively. We recommend introducing heading to players who are 6 years of age or older but leaving the decision of whether or not to head the ball during games to the individual player. Some of your players who are 6, 7, 8, and 9 years old will head a ball during a game, providing it comes fairly gently to them. Others will not be ready to head in a game and should not be forced to head until they are experienced and confident. Generally, players 10 years and older who have developed heading skills will want to head in games.

For those players over 10 years who are still apprehensive, your task as a coach is to provide fun practices and encouragement so they can develop the skill and the confidence to head effectively.

Most players who are 13 years and older should be ready for heading in the game, providing they feel confident about performing the skill. But even then, heading is a personal preference and, just as some players are better dribblers than others, some players are better at heading than others. Therefore, place players who are good at heading the ball in positions where they can use this skill and players who do not excel at heading in positions where they are not often required to head during the game.

Heading Fundamentals and Teaching Progression

Heading is a relatively challenging skill that, if not taught correctly, may cause discomfort for young players. Many young players do not have the neck strength to head a fast flying ball several times. Therefore, we recommend you follow the previously stated suggestions for heading in games and teach your players each of the following heading fundamentals. This will ensure that your players learn the skill correctly, develop the strength and coordination needed to head, and reduce the risk of injury. The Head With Partner Drill (5.2), Head Juggle (5.3), and the Wall Heading Drill (5.5) are great activities to practice heading fundamentals.

Legs, Trunk, and Neck Provide Support and Power

Because the head contacts the ball, the rest of the body must help support and stabilize the head. Ask your players to move the head as far as possible in every direction. Notice that the head can turn from side to side and tilt forward and back, but cannot by itself head the ball with much power. Consequently, the first fundamental to

teach your players is that *the legs, trunk, and neck provide support and power to head the ball.*

Demonstrate how to spread the legs apart about shoulder width, in a slight front to back position, as shown in Figure 5-1. This stance provides a solid base of support from which players can push into the ball. Raising the arms slightly away from the side will help players maintain balance.

Fig. 5-1

Lean Back, Then Push and Throw Head Into Ball

The second fundamental to teach your players is that, even with a good base of support, they will not head the ball with power unless they *lean back, then push and throw the head into the ball* (see Figure 5-2). As the ball arrives, players need to (a) bend the legs and lean back slightly, then (b) tighten the stomach, neck, and shoulders against the force of the ball, and (c) push with the legs and throw the head into the ball.

Fig. 5-2

Watch the Ball and Contact at Forehead

The third fundamental to teach your players is that they must *continually watch the ball* and *must contact the ball at the forehead* (see Figure 5-3). If players close their eyes or turn their heads to look at something else, they will not be in position to head the ball. If the ball falls in a way different from the way they expected or if their heads are turned, they will be unable to adjust their positions. We recommend that you tell your players to watch the ball until it reaches the head, keeping their eyes open. Also, the top and side of the head are not as strong as the forehead and players may experience short-term discomfort if the ball hits these surfaces.

Fig. 5-3

Coaching Points for Heading Fundamentals

1. Develop a strong base of support and power by spreading the legs and raising the arms.
2. Develop power to head the ball by bending the legs and leaning back slightly, then pushing and throwing the head into the ball.
3. Tighten the stomach, neck, and shoulders.
4. Watch the ball all the way to the head and contact at the forehead.

Heading Forward

This technique is used in passing, scoring goals, and clearing the ball in defense. It is the easiest type of heading to learn first, because the head does not have to redirect the ball; the ball is headed back in the direction it came from, in front of the body. Use the following coaching points to teach your players how to head the ball forward:

- Head through the ball by "throwing" the head at the ball. Make sure the head hits the ball rather than the ball hitting the head.
- Use the legs to propel the trunk, neck, and head forward to meet the ball.
- Follow through with the forehead for maximum power.
- Head high by heading under the middle of the ball and head down by heading above the middle of the ball (see Figure 5-4).

Fig. 5-4

Heading Sideways

Many times your players will want to head the ball sideways to pass to another player or to score a goal. Explain that heading sideways does not mean using the side of the head. Instead, the upper body, neck, and head turn toward the target, and the head redirects the ball. Use the following coaching points and Figure 5-5 to teach your players how to head the ball to the side:

- Players turn the head and body to redirect the ball toward the target.
- Follow through by continuing to push the head in the direction you are heading the ball, even after making contact.

- Tell your players to imagine that a piece of string is tied to the middle of their forehead and that on contact with the ball this piece of string pulls their head to redirect the ball.

Fig. 5-5

Heading Backward

Sometimes your players will need to head the ball in the direction that it is already going but opposite from the way they are facing. This is often used in offensive play when a ball is passed at head height from a goalkeeper's kick to a forward or from a throw-in or corner kick. This can be done in two ways. When possible, players can turn to the side and head the ball sideways. But, when players do not have enough time to turn and prepare to head sideways, they can judge the flight of the ball and, facing the ball, head with a quick backward *flick* of the head (see Figure 5-6).

Fig. 5-6

This is an advanced technique that should be taught to players who have mastered basic heading techniques. In addition to the activities listed earlier, Heading Circle (5.4) and Heading Pepper (5.6) are excellent activities to practice heading forward, backward, and sideways. Use the following coaching points to teach players to head backward.

- Imagine your forehead is attached to a piece of string that is pulled back as soon as the ball makes contact.
- Make contact with the forehead on the lower side of the ball beneath the midline.
- The head follows through backward.

Heading in the Air

Well-skilled players will sometimes want to jump and head a ball from a corner kick, goal kick, or throw-in. Because the player leaves the ground, the legs no longer provide a base of support; all of the support must come from the trunk, shoulders, and neck. Also, all of the power must come from the momentum generated during the jump and from the flexing action of the trunk and neck. Use the following coaching points to teach players to head in the air.

- Jump to meet the ball, and time the jump so that the ball is headed at the peak of the jump (see Figure 5-7).

Fig. 5-7

- Use the trunk, shoulders, and neck to generate power.
- Raise the arms to maintain balance.
- Tighten the neck and shoulders as the trunk and neck push the head into the ball.

Teaching Progression for Heading

1. Teach players how to head initially using soft, light balls, and progressing to regulation soccer balls.
2. Teach players to form a solid base of support by spreading the legs and standing with the feet staggered in a front to back position.
3. Teach players to prepare for the ball by leaning back and bending the legs slightly.
4. Teach players to tighten the muscles of the stomach, neck, and shoulders as they contact the ball.
5. Teach players to watch the ball until it reaches the head and to contact the ball at the forehead.
6. Teach players how to head the ball forward and sideways.
7. Teach players who have mastered fundamental heading skills to head backward and to jump and head in the air.

Games and Activities for Heading

Heading in actual games can be quite different from heading in practices. We recommend that you include games that allow players to practice heading against opponents in competitive situations, such as Heading Keep-Away (5.7) and Headed Goals Only (5.9).

(5.1) Discover the Heading Surface

Purpose. To introduce the heading surface and allow young players to develop a feel for heading the ball.

Organization. Spread players comfortably apart, with one ball for each player.

Directions. Show players how to hold the ball with both hands, extend the head forward, and bring the ball onto the forehead (see Figure 5-8). Point out that the ball should meet the head at the hairline of the forehead. Initially, have players head with the ball in the hands. Gradually progress to having them head the ball out of the hands and into the air. Finally, have players toss the ball a few feet in the air, head into the air, and catch the ball.

Fig. 5-8

(5.2) Head With Partner

Purpose. To practice heading fundamentals.

Organization. Players can work alone or in groups of two or three, with one ball per single player or per group.

Directions. Partners stand 6 to 10 ft apart and alternate tossing and heading the ball forward or sideways. As players become more experienced, they can head the ball to each other rather than tossing it. Have contests to see which group can head the ball the greatest number of times. In groups of three, players can also practice heading backward.

(5.3) Head Juggle

Purpose. To practice heading fundamentals.

Organization. Players spread out across the field, with one ball per player.

Directions. This game is a more challenging version of (5.1) Discover the Heading Surface.

Players toss, head, and catch until they can control the ball well. Then progress to heading twice and three times before catching. See how many times players can head the ball.

(5.4) Heading Circle

Purpose. To practice heading skills.

Organization. Divide players into groups of five or more players, with one ball per group. Players form a circle with one player in the center.

Directions. This game has several variations:

1. The player in the center can toss the ball to other players, who head it back.
2. Players around the circle can toss the ball to the center player who heads it back.
3. Players try to head the ball back and forth around the circle without catching or dropping it.
4. All players stand in the circle, call out the name of a player, and head the ball to him or her without catching or dropping it.

(5.5) Wall Heading

Purpose. To practice heading forward, sideways, and backward.

Organization. Players can work alone or in groups of two or three, with one ball per player or per group.

Directions. Players toss and head balls at a wall. In groups of two or three, players can practice heading sideways while a partner retrieves the ball. Encourage players to select a target spot on the wall and hit it with the ball.

(5.6) Heading Pepper

Purpose. To practice heading skills.

Organization. Divide players into groups of four or more, with one ball per group. One player is the passer and stands 6 to 10 ft in front of the others who stand side to side in a line (see Figure 5-9).

Directions. Similar to Pepper (3.5). The passer heads the ball to teammates who head it back. If the passer makes a mistake, he or she loses the turn and moves to the end of the line, and the player at the front of the line becomes the passer. If a player in the line misheads, he or she loses that spot and moves to the end of the line.

Fig. 5-9

(5.7) Heading Keep-Away

Purpose. To practice heading against opponents.

Organization. Divide the team into groups of three, with one ball per group. Two of the players stand 15 to 20 ft apart, with the third player positioned between them.

Directions. Players at each end alternate tossing and heading over the player in the middle, who tries to head the ball away. When the middle player does intercept, he or she switches positions with the player who tossed the ball.

(5.8) Heading Sit-Ups

Purpose. To practice using the back and neck in heading.

Organization. Pair up players, with one ball per pair. One player sits on the ground with his or her hands and feet off the ground. The partner holds the ball and stands about 10 ft away facing the sitting player.

Directions. The sitting player lies back and does a sit-up to head the ball back to the partner. The partner should toss the ball easily at head height for the sitting player. Emphasize the use of the back and neck in the heading action, and encourage good service form using an underhand toss.

(5.9) Headed Goals Only

Purpose. To practice heading at the goal in a game situation.

Organization. Divide players into two equal teams for a scrimmage game.

Directions. Play a regular scrimmage game, but mark a 10- by 10-yd square on each side of the penalty area (see Figure 5-10). Only offensive players can enter these areas by dribbling or by receiving a pass. When in this area, players can throw-in the ball to teammates who can score only by heading.

Fig. 5-10

(5.10) Heading Backward

Purpose. To practice heading backward.

Organization. Divide players into groups of three, and place them in a straight line about 8 to 9 yd apart, with one ball per group.

Directions. One player at the end of the line serves a ball, throw-in style, at the head of the middle player who heads it backward to the player at the other end of the line. The ball should be served with a flat throw to make it easier to flick the ball backward with the forehead.

(5.11) Throw, Head, and Catch

Purpose. To practice heading in different directions during a game.

Organization. Divide your players into teams of five or six and mark a field 50 by 40 yd.

Directions. Play a small-sided scrimmage game where both teams have to advance the ball downfield with a throw, head, catch sequence. One player throws the ball to a teammate to head so that another teammate can catch the ball. Encourage players with developed receiving and controlling skills to receive the ball with the body, legs, or feet, rather than to catch it. The opposing team can intercept headers but not the initial throw. Goals can be scored only by headers.

Chapter 6: Scoring Goals

Introduction: Scoring Is Everything

As in most team sports, the team that scores the most goals wins. Unlike in some other sports, however, in soccer few goals are likely to be scored each game. Typical scores range from 1–0 to 3–2, which is not much scoring compared to basketball or football. Consequently, in game play every goal is important and could be the winner. Scoring should also be an important part of your practice sessions. Players love to score goals and will be enthusiastic about practices that involve scoring. If you notice that your players are becoming bored, you can liven up the session by practicing shots on the goal.

When your players practice scoring goals, be sure they try scoring from all possible situations. Practice long shots, short tap-in shots, chip shots, and headers. Practice with a goalkeeper and other defenders so players can experience the variety of situations that will exist in games. Soccer is a dynamic game with rapidly changing situations. At one second the goalkeeper may be near the left corner, when a shot to the right would score. At the next second, the goalkeeper may be in the center of the goal but well away from the goal line, when a shot to the right would be stopped but a chip shot might score. Players must learn to read these options and take the most opportune shot.

Scoring goals requires effective ball control and knowledge of when to shoot, when not to shoot, how to shoot, and where to shoot. No perfect method of scoring exists, only guidelines or principles to help players consider offensive playing strategies or tactics. These principles (presented in chapter 11) also help players work together as a unit and determine the best shot for each situation. Because every player is a potential scoring threat, all players, even defensive players, must learn these principles. This chapter presents suggestions about teaching scoring principles to your players, fun games to help players practice them, and the following specific principles for effective scoring:

- Principle 1: Take the Opportunity
- Principle 2: Determine the Best Shooting Technique
- Principle 3: Shoot From a Good Angle
- Principle 4: Shoot Low and Away From the Goalkeeper
- Principle 5: Create Space for Scoring Opportunities
- Principle 6: Follow All Shots

Principle 1: Take the Opportunity

Players often miss opportunities to score because they want to get in a better position to pass the ball to a teammate who is open, or they are afraid to shoot with their nondominant foot. The first principle of effective scoring that you should teach your players is *shoot at every opportunity*. Remember to emphasize that soccer is a low scoring game, so every reasonable shot should be taken.

Deciding which shots are reasonable is the dilemma most players face. If they score a goal they are heroes, but the thought of missing and being reprimanded by the coach and viewed negatively by spectators is sometimes strong enough to dissuade players from shooting at all. You can encourage your players to take advantage of every opportunity to score by creating an enjoyable and nonthreatening atmosphere at practice sessions. Encourage players to shoot with their nondominant foot, reward hustle and effort, and don't reprimand players for shooting inaccurately with the nondominant foot. Players should not be afraid to make mistakes in practices or games. Everyone makes mistakes, and mistakes help us learn. Rapid Fire (6.1) is a fun game that will help players learn to take advantage of scoring opportunities.

Principle 2: Determine the Best Shooting Technique

The second principle of effective shooting that you should teach your players is *determine the best shooting technique*. The type of shot needed to score a goal depends upon (a) whether the ball is on the ground or in the air, (b) the distance from the goal, and (c) the position of the goalkeeper.

If the ball is on the ground, the instep or the laces should be used to shoot. If the ball is in the air, a volley or header should be used. Generally,

Fig. 6-1

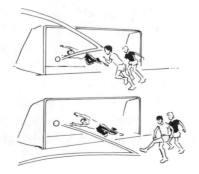

use a header for balls above the waist and a volley kick for balls below the waist (see Figure 6-1).

The farther from the goal a shot is taken, the more power is needed to push it past the goalkeeper. Conversely, the closer to the goal the shot is taken the less power and the more accuracy is needed to place the ball past the goalkeeper. Also, remind your players that the more powerful the shot, the less control the shooter has over it.

If the goalkeeper is on the goal line, a straight shot to the corners will be more effective than a high, arching shot. If the goalie moves too far away from the goal line, however, a chip shot over the head or curve shot around the side is better than a straight shot (see Figure 6-2).

Fig. 6-2

Principle 3: Shoot From a Good Angle

The angle of a shot is an important factor in deciding when to shoot. Shots from the side of the goal or at acute angles require more accuracy and are less likely to score than shots taken from a more direct angle (see Figure 6-3). Therefore, the third scoring principle to teach your players is *shoot from a good angle*. Demonstrate shots from good angles and explain how the chances for scoring change as the angle of the shot changes. The game Shooting From a Distance (6.2) will help players learn shooting angles and how to place shots past defenders.

Fig. 6-3

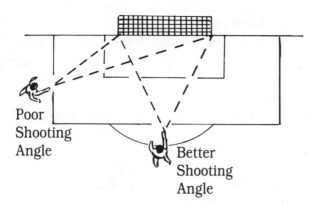

Teach players that shots taken closer to the goal are more effective than shots taken farther from the goal. The farther away an attacker takes a shot, the more time goalkeepers and other defenders have to react to the shot and to stop the ball. Also, teach players to assess each goal scoring situation. For example, if a player has a chance to shoot from a poor shooting angle, encourage him or her to check to see if there is a teammate in a better scoring position and, if so, to pass to that open teammate.

Principle 4:
Shoot Low and Away
From the Goalkeeper

In addition to shooting from a good angle, players should try to shoot as far from the goalkeeper as possible. Also, players should make shots that force the goalkeeper to move out of position to stop the ball. Shooting low and toward the corner, rather than in the air, causes the goalkeeper to bend over, kneel, or dive, reducing his or her mobility and forcing him or her to take longer to reach the ball. Therefore, the fourth general principle to teach your players is *shoot low and away from the goalie* (see Figure 6-4).

An effective method to demonstrate this is to let all of your players practice goalkeeping, tossing a variety of shots to them. They will discover that shots close to them and in the air are easier

to stop than shots farther from them and low to the ground.

Fig. 6-4

Principle 5:
Create Space
for Scoring Opportunities

Typically, offensive players bunch together near the goal where they are closely marked by defenders. This tendency does not facilitate scoring. Instead, it helps the defense, because controlling and shooting the ball is more difficult when offensive players are bunched together. Teach your players the fifth principle of effective shooting, to *create space for scoring opportunities*. Show players how to spread out to open the area near the goal, then to dribble to that open area for a shot, or how to pass to players cutting through for a shot (see Figure 6-5). Techniques on creating space and other offensive tactics are presented in chapter 9.

Fig. 6-5

Principle 6:
Follow All Shots

Many goals are scored, after blocked shots, by players who understand the sixth principle for effective scoring: *follow each shot* (see Figure 6-6). This point is easy to state and easy for players to understand, but it is difficult to execute. Players tend to shoot and watch the ball, not realizing that the defenders have switched their attention from trying to mark them to trying to stop the ball. Consequently, offensive players are usually free to follow the ball and usually in a good position to shoot again if the ball is deflected or dropped by the goalkeeper. Playing Small-Sided Scrimmage Games (6.6) is a fun and effective way to practice shooting against the goalkeeper, creating space to score, and following shots.

Fig. 6-6

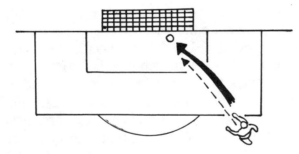

Coaching Points
for Scoring Goals

1. Encourage players to shoot whenever possible, using each shooting technique.
2. Develop shooting skills in practices by creating an enjoyable atmosphere in which players are not afraid to makes mistakes and can gain confidence.
3. Learn to volley or shoot with the head when the ball is in the air and with all surfaces of the foot when the ball is on the ground.
4. For balls above the waist, shoot with the head. For balls below the waist, shoot with a volley kick.

5. Shoot from a good angle, in front or slightly to the side of the goal, rather than near the goal line.
6. Shoot where the goalkeeper is least likely to stop the ball, i.e., shoot low and away from the goalkeeper.
7. Continue the attack by following every shot, looking for balls that are deflected or dropped.

Teaching Progression
for Scoring Goals

1. Teach players to shoot often, whenever they have a reasonable shot.
2. Teach players to determine the best shooting technique.
3. Teach players to shoot from a good angle.
4. Teach players to shoot low and away from the goalkeeper.
5. Teach players to create space for scoring opportunities.
6. Teach players to follow every shot.

Games and Activities
for Scoring Goals

(6.1) Rapid Fire

Purpose. To practice scoring goals without defenders.

Organization. Position players at the top of the penalty area. Coaches stand inside the penalty area and off to one side (see Figure 6-7). Each player has a ball.

Directions. Begin with one player as the goalkeeper and one as the shooter. You toss or pass the ball to the shooter, varying the serve so players must practice different shots (straight, lofted, chip, head, volley, etc.). Be sure that players practice shooting from the right side, left side, and directly in front of goal. After the shot, the shooter assumes the position of goalie, the previous goalie retrieves the ball and moves to the end of the line, and the player at the beginning of the line becomes the shooter. As an option, players can try to dribble and beat the goalkeeper. To make it more challenging, have players dribble around a course of cones before shooting.

Fig. 6-7

(6.2) Shooting From a Distance

Purpose. To practice longer shots against opponents.

Organization. Divide players into teams of four. Two teams play against each other at one end of the field, with one ball per every two teams. Position the defensive team inside the penalty area and the offensive team outside the penalty area, or mark the field into two even halves with a goal at either end.

Directions. The offensive team spreads out and shoots from within their area. The defensive team tries to block the shot without leaving their area. If the ball is stopped, but bounces back to the offensive team, the offensive team can shoot again. If the defensive team stops the shot, it tosses it back to the offensive team. Teams switch positions after three attempts. Encourage players to pass the ball until there is a gap between defensive players for a shot. A slight variation that makes this a fast-paced game is to mark a goal area at the back of each team's area. If one team shoots but does not score, the other team controls the ball and tries to shoot. This helps players make the transition from offense to defense, and vice versa.

(6.3) Shooting in Groups of Five

Purpose. To practice shooting fundamentals.

Organization. Divide the players into groups of five; four players shoot and one player plays goalkeeper, with one ball per group. Use cones or other markers to form two 20- by 20-yd grids; in between the grids mark a goal area (see Figure 6-8). Position two players in each side of the playing area.

Directions. Players on each side of the goal alternate shooting at the goal. If the ball goes through the goal, players on the other side control the ball and pass to shoot. Rotate the goalkeeper every five shots.

Fig. 6-8

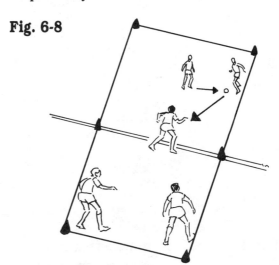

(6.4) Cut-Throat

Purpose. To practice shooting under pressure.

Organization. Divide the team into groups of four; one player is goalkeeper while the other three play against each other, with one ball per group. Use cones or other objects to mark a 30- by 30-yd playing area in front of the goal.

Directions. The goalkeeper begins play by tossing the ball into the playing area to one player. The objects of the drill are for the player with the ball to score, and for the players without the ball to defend and try to win the ball so they can score. Each time a goal is scored, the goalkeeper tosses the ball to a different player, until three goals are scored by one player. The goalkeeper then switches with the player that scored three goals.

(6.5) Shootout

Purpose. To practice scoring against the goalkeeper when clear from the defense.

Organization. Arrange players in front of the goal area, as shown in Figure 6-9. Designate one player as goalkeeper and one as attacking player. The attacking player should begin the attack about 30 yd from the goal.

Directions. Players dribble toward the goal and try to beat the goalkeeper and push a shot into the goal. After each shot the goalkeeper retrieves the ball and the attacking player becomes the goalkeeper.

Fig. 6-9

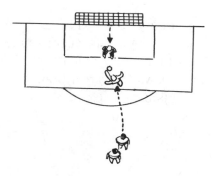

(6.6) Small-Sided Scrimmage Games

Purpose. To practice scoring goals in competitive situations.

Organization. Divide teams into groups of three or four players, with one ball per every two teams. Your regular goalkeeper can play his usual position, or you can rotate one player as the goalkeeper after each game.

Directions. Teams play against each other for 5 to 10 min. Rotate teams and begin more games.

You can vary this game to play any combination of defenders vs attackers, for example, 3 vs 2, 3 vs 3, 5 vs 3.

Variations:

Three Versus One to Goal is designed to have players practice moving the ball and shooting at the goal under moderate pressure. Divide the team into groups of six players. One player is the goalkeeper, one player plays defense, three players are attackers, and one player retrieves shots (see Figure 6-10). The defensive player begins by passing the ball to the attacking players. The attackers then try to beat the defender and score past the goalkeeper. Rotate positions after every three shots.

Fig. 6-10

Six Versus Four is designed to practice shooting under competitive conditions. Position six offensive players and four defensive players in one half of the field, and a goalkeeper in front of the goal. The offense begins from the midfield line and tries to score, while the defense tries to stop the shot and win the ball. If using four defenders makes it too difficult for players to score, play six versus three.

Chapter 7: Goalkeeping

Introduction: A Unique Position

Although every other player on a soccer team kicks, heads, and controls the ball without hands, the goalkeeper jumps and dives after the ball and uses his or her hands to push or catch it. Using the hands makes goalkeeping a unique function in soccer, and goalkeepers are a minority on teams. Usually only two or three players on a team specialize at that position. Practice time is often devoted to developing skills for the majority of players; this may result in your neglecting the development of your goalkeepers' skills. We suggest that you encourage all players to learn goalkeeping skills and provide time each practice for goalkeepers to practice their specific skills. Not everyone will want to keep goal, but everyone should have the opportunity.

Goalkeepers can use their hands only while inside the penalty area and, to avoid having anyone confuse goalkeepers with other players, goalkeepers wear colors different from either team. If goalkeepers play outside the penalty area, they must conform to rules required of any other player and cannot use their hands.

The following topics are presented in this chapter to help you teach goalkeeping to your players:

- Goalkeeper's Equipment
- Movement Fundamentals
- Positioning in the Goal
- Handling and Collecting Techniques
- Throwing and Punting Techniques
- Teaching Progression for Goalkeeping
- Games and Activities for Goalkeeping

Goalkeeper's Equipment

Because goalkeepers jump, dive, and fall to stop shots, it is important they wear proper protective clothing, especially when playing on hard surfaces. Special shirts, shorts, pants, and gloves are made exclusively for goalkeepers (see Figure 7-1). Goalkeepers should wear long-sleeved shirts with padded elbows to protect their arms and elbows. Shorts and pants should be padded at the hips to protect against bruises, grazes, and burns from falling on turf or hard ground. Some pants have special pads for the knees, and kneepads can be purchased separately.

Fig. 7-1

Movement Fundamentals

Because the soccer goal is 8 yd wide, goalkeepers must be prepared to dive, jump, run sideways or toward the ball, quickly. Thus, balance and agility are two important qualities that goalkeepers should develop. Even the quickest player, however, will not be able to stop a good shot if he or she does not know how to prepare to move, how to move to the side, and how to move toward the ball to reduce the shooting angle. Goalkeeper Shuffle (7.1), Rapid Fire (7.2), and Goalkeeper Agility and Reaction Exercises (7.3) are effective games to help players develop movement fundamentals.

Goalkeeper's Stance

Teaching goalkeepers a *ready position* or *stance* is quite important; it is also a bit of a dilemma. Because every person is different, and because scoring situations change from moment to moment, every person needs to develop his or her own ready position. However, every person should include the following movement principles in his or her stance (see Figure 7-2).

Fig. 7-2

- Spread the legs comfortably to form a base of support, with the feet aligned.
- Bend at the knees and place most of the weight on the balls of the feet. This will help players shift body weight and move in any direction quickly. Some players may feel more comfortable moving their feet up and down or bouncing slightly.
- Spread the hands and hold them to each side of the body at about chest level. This will help players maintain balance and reach the ball quickly.

Moving Sideways

The most effective method for moving sideways over short distances is to *sidestep*. Following Figure 7-3, demonstrate how to shift the feet from side to side without crossing them. This is an effective method for moving prior to a shot or when retrieving slow-rolling balls.

Fig. 7-3

Jumping to Save High Balls

Proper positioning in the goal and proper movement fundamentals will reduce the need to jump and dive after balls, but from time to time a good jump or dive could be the difference between a save or a goal. Young people learn to jump as they grow up, but they do not learn how to catch in the air and how to land while clutching a ball. Following Figure 7-4, teach your players to jump by (a) taking two or three steps and jumping as high as possible off one preferred foot and (b) raising the knee of the nonjumping leg, reaching up with the arms. Raising the knee provides additional momentum, increasing the height of the jump and providing protection from attackers.

Fig. 7-4

Diving

A goalkeeper making a diving save is an exciting and spectacular sight. It requires excellent timing, athletic ability, and courage. Good footwork and proper positioning reduce the need to dive for balls, but there will always be the need to dive to save shots. Diving is an advanced skill, however, that should be taught and practiced only when your players are physically able and skilled enough to dive well.

Teach and practice diving on safe, soft surfaces, such as thick grass that is free of hazards. Encourage players to wear long-sleeved shirts and long pants when practicing dives. For games, goalkeepers should wear protective clothing that has padding built into the knees and elbows.

As shown in Figure 7-5, teach your players to dive using the following progression that is also used in the Dive Progression Drill (7.4):

Fig. 7-5

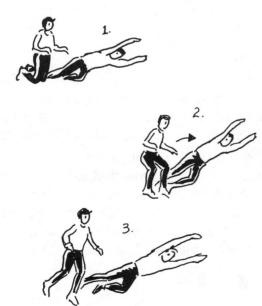

1. Begin with players on their knees with their hands up in the ready position. Then have players fall to the side on the fleshy part of their hips and shoulders, with their chests facing the field of play and their elbows tucked into their sides. Have them practice

landing on the right side of the body and on the left side of the body, first without the ball, then with the ball.

2. After your players feel comfortable landing from their knees, have them practice landing from a squat. Again, have players practice landing on both sides of the body without the ball and then with the ball.

3. After your players feel comfortable landing from a squatting position, have them practice landing from a full upright, ready position. Again, have players practice landing on both sides of the body without the ball, then with the ball.

There are two ways that players can catch a ball while diving. The first method is to have the player catch the ball, secure it to the chest, and roll away from attackers to protect himself or herself and the ball (see Figure 7-6). The second method is for the player to catch the ball with one hand behind the ball, one hand on top, trapping it against the ground (which acts as a third hand) (see Figure 7-7). Then the player can roll away from the attackers.

Fig. 7-6

Fig. 7-7

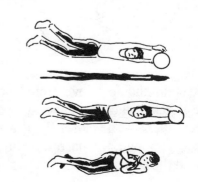

Coaching Points for Movement Fundamentals

1. Stand comfortably, with knees slightly bent and weight balanced on the balls of the feet and with hands held at about chest height.
2. Sidestep, without crossing the feet, to move sideways over short distances.
3. Jump and land on the toes and roll to the heels.
4. Cushion dives with the shoulders and thigh.
5. Secure the ball by clutching it to the chest or by trapping it against the ground and then rolling away from attackers.

Positioning in the Goal

An important part of playing goalkeeper is correct *positioning in the goal*. Goalkeepers should play 1 or 2 yd in front of the goal line to stop balls early. Also, goalkeepers should always face the ball and cover as much of the goal area as possible. For example, when the ball is off to the side, the shooting angle is changed, and the shot must come from an angle near the side (see Figure 7-8). Therefore, goalkeepers should play toward the side of the goal and cover the post nearest the ball. As the ball moves from one side of the goal to the other, the goalkeeper should move from side to side.

Fig. 7-8

A goalkeeper should move from the goal toward the attacker when he or she is one-on-one against the attacker. The closer the goalkeeper moves toward the ball, the narrower the shooting angle and the easier it is to stop the shot (see

Figure 7-9). Demonstrate that goalkeepers should be agile and should "play low" to be ready to drop to the ground and save the ball.

Fig. 7-9

Handling and Collecting Techniques

Your goalkeepers must know how to stop the ball once they reach it. The methods for stopping shots are to *catch and collect the ball* and to *deflect the ball* by punching or pushing it with the hands. To help your players develop catching and deflecting skills, practice Ball Handling Exercises (7.5), Collect and Squeeze (7.6), and Think Fast (7.7)

Collecting Shots

The techniques used to collect or catch shots depend upon the position of the ball. In every case, goalkeepers should (a) move in line with the ball, (b) catch the ball with both hands, and (c) pull the ball to the chest to secure it.

- Shots on the ground should be caught by bending down, placing the hands behind the ball with the fingers pointing down, scooping the ball into the arms, and securing it to the chest while standing (see Figure 7-10).

Fig. 7-10

• Shots in the air and below the waist should be caught with the hands down, bending to catch the ball at about waist height, and securing it to the chest while standing (see Figure 7-11).

Fig. 7-11

• Shots in the air and above the waist should be caught with the hands up and behind the ball with fingers pointing up and the thumbs close together (see Figure 7-12).

Fig. 7-12

Deflecting Shots

Sometimes shots will be so fast, high, or to the side that your goalkeeper cannot catch the ball. In these situations, goalkeepers can punch or push shots away from the goal. Demonstrate that to punch the ball, players should make a fist (see Figure 7-13a) and hit the ball with one or two hands (see Figure 7-13b). To push the ball, players should use an open hand, guiding the ball away from the goal (see Figure 7-14). Explain

that they should direct shots that are near the side of the goal beyond the side post and shots that are near the top of the goal over the goal.

Fig. 7-13a

Fig. 7-13b

Fig. 7-14

Coaching Points for Collecting and Deflecting Shots

1. Move in line with the ball.
2. Catch balls with the hands and clutch them to the chest.

3. Catch balls below the waist with hands down. Catch balls above the waist with hands up.
4. Punch shots with fists and push shots with open hands.
5. Punch or push shots to the side or over the goal.

Throwing and Punting Techniques

Goalkeepers are usually considered defensive players, but they are also important to a team's offense. After catching a shot, the goalie initiates the offense by passing the ball to teammates. A method of initiating the offense and maintaining control of the ball is to *throw* the ball to teammates near the goal. A method of initiating the offense by passing the ball over a longer distance is to *punt* the ball. Punting may appear to be more advantageous than throwing, because the ball moves quickly toward the opponents' goal. Remind your players, however, that it is difficult to receive and control long passes and that long passes can be easily intercepted by the opposing team. On the other hand, short, controlled throws may seem less advantageous than punts because the ball is close to the goal. Controlled passes, though, are easier for teammates to receive and the offense can then advance the ball upfield effectively. No matter how players pass, tell them to throw to the side of the goal. Passing directly in front of the goal is dangerous, because if the ball is stolen, the opposing team usually has a direct shot at the goal. Throw and Punt (7.8) will keep each player active and provide the practice needed to learn how to throw and punt balls from the goal area.

Throwing

Goalkeepers can throw the ball using three different techniques: (a) *bowling* or *underhand style*, (b) *baseball pass* or *overhand style*, and (c) *sideways* or *round-arm style*.

The bowling technique is used to pass the ball in a smooth fashion over short distances. It provides an easy pass for teammates to control. Use this technique only when no defenders are near. Demonstrate how to bowl by (a) holding the ball in two hands, (b) swinging the ball back with one hand, and (c) striding forward with the opposite foot as the player bends to the ground and swings the ball forward (see Figure 7-15).

Fig. 7-15

Demonstrate the baseball throw by throwing the ball overhand as you would throw a baseball (see Figure 7-16). With this technique, players can throw the ball farther from the goal than with the bowling technique, but the baseball pass is not as accurate and easy to receive as the bowling technique. A common error is swinging the arm completely across the body, which causes the ball to curve. Point out that keeping the thumb down as the ball is thrown will help the ball fly straight rather than curve.

Fig. 7-16

The round-arm technique is used to hurl the ball farther than the baseball technique and should be used to clear the ball to teammates (see Figure 7-17). Show players how to throw from the side by (a) wrapping the hand around the ball, (b) taking a long stride forward, and (c) whipping the ball with a straight arm over the top of the head.

Fig. 7-17

Punting

The most effective use of punting the ball to the opponents' side is to catch them off-guard and attack quickly, particularly when kicking with the wind. Explain that goalkeepers should punt the ball from the air, similar to a volley, or punt the ball as it bounces, similar to a half-volley (see Figure 7-18 and 7-19). A punt from the air will fly higher than a punt from the ground.

Fig. 7-18

Fig. 7-19

To punt from the air, players should (a) hold the ball in both hands, (b) take a long stride with the nonkicking foot, (c) drop the ball in front of the nonkicking foot, and (d) kick with the top of the foot. To punt as the ball bounces, follow this procedure but time the kick so the foot contacts the ball as it bounces.

Coaching Points for Throwing and Punting

1. Use the bowling technique to throw easy, controlled passes to teammates near the goal.
2. Use the baseball technique to pass to teammates who are a moderate distance from the goal.
3. Use the round-arm technique to pass the ball over long distances.
4. Punt from the air, similar to a volley, to pass the ball high and long.
5. Punt from the ground, similar to a half-volley, to pass the ball low to the ground and long.

Teaching Progression for Goalkeeping

1. Introduce goalkeepers to proper clothing and equipment and warn against the dangers of not wearing such clothing.
2. Teach goalkeepers how to prepare to stop shots and how to move forward and sideways.
3. Teach goalkeepers how to jump and dive to stop shots.
4. Teach goalkeepers to adjust to the rapidly changing ball positions.
5. Teach goalkeepers to always face the ball, to play toward the goalpost nearest the ball, and to play toward the center when the ball is toward the center.
6. Teach goalkeepers to reduce the shooting angle by moving toward the ball when in a one-on-one situation against an attacker.
7. Teach goalkeepers to collect shots by moving in front of the ball, catching it, and clutching it to the chest.

8. Teach players to punch or push the ball to the side of the goal or over the goal only when they are unable to catch it.

9. Teach players to initiate the offense by throwing or punting the ball to teammates.

Games and Activities for Goalkeeping

(7.1) Goalkeeper Shuffle

Purpose. To practice moving in different directions and positioning oneself in the goal area.

Organization. Mark several 10- by 10-yd grids and divide the team into groups of three, with one ball per group. Select one player as goalkeeper, one as caller, and one as shooter. The goalkeeper stands on one side of grid, the caller stands to the side, and the shooter stands at the side opposite the goalkeeper.

Directions. The caller directs the position of the shooter by calling "right," "center," or "left," and the goalkeeper moves with the ball to protect the goal. When the caller shouts "shoot," the shooter is free to score, and the goalkeeper should move toward the ball to reduce the shooting angle. The caller moves to shooter position, the shooter moves to goalkeeper position, and the goalkeeper moves to caller position. For older players, play on a regulation field with three shooters who pass the ball around the penalty area. When "shoot" is called, the player with the ball tries to score against the goalkeeper.

(7.2) Rapid Fire

Purpose. To develop goalkeeper movement and reaction skills.

Organization. Set out three cones in a triangle formation 8 yd apart to form three goalmouths (see Figure 7-20a), or four cones in a line in front of a fence to keep balls from rolling away (see Figure 7-20b). Divide your team into groups of four players. One player is the goalkeeper, the other players are shooters.

Directions. In sequence each player shoots at the goal, as the goalkeeper tries to catch or deflect

the shot, then moves on to the next goal. Players rotate positions after every three or four sequences. Players can keep track of the number of shots they collect or deflect as a competitive game.

Fig. 7-20a

Fig. 7-20b

(7.3) Goalkeeper Agility and Reaction Exercises

Purpose. To develop movement skills, anticipation, and coordination needed to collect and deflect shots.

Organization. Pair up players or practice with goalkeepers separately. Position each pair in a grid or practice with goalkeepers in front of the goal.

Directions. Each agility and reaction exercise is unique, and you must evaluate how effective each is for your players. Procedures for each exercise are listed below.

- One player bounces the ball hard on the ground, and the goalkeeper leaps to catch it above the head. Rotate after every 10 bounces. Be sure players secure collected balls to the chest.

- One player tosses balls to either side of the goalkeeper, and the goalkeeper hustles to collect or deflect the ball. Rotate after every 10 tosses. Be sure players secure the collected balls to the chest.
- The goalkeeper lies on his or her back while the partner tosses or bounces the ball high in the air. When the ball is at the highest point, the partner calls "Go!" and the goalkeeper tries to stand and catch the ball. Rotate after every 10 tosses.
- The goalkeeper lies on his or her stomach in the "push-up" position in front of the goal or the goal area marked inside a grid. The partner tosses or passes the ball high and low to either side. Goalkeeper tries to get up and collect or deflect the ball. Having a large supply of balls helps this exercise keep moving.
- Divide the team into groups of at least three players. One player is goalkeeper, the other two players are feeders or shooters. Feeders stand 15 to 20 yd from the goalkeeper and toss or shoot the ball to the sides of the goal. The goalkeeper tries to collect or deflect the ball, retrieves it, and moves to the end of the line. The shooter then becomes the goalkeeper. You can have each player count the number of balls he or she catches or deflects. The player with the greatest number wins.

(7.4) Dive Progression

Purpose. To practice diving after balls. This should be played by players older than 10 years.

Directions. This progression has three stages. First, players kneel and fall to each side to experience hitting the ground. Second, players crouch or squat and dive easily to each side to experience hitting the ground, initially without stepping to the side, then with stepping to the side. Third, players stand in the ready position, sidestep, and dive. This drill requires you to decide which players are capable of safely performing at each stage. Do not force players to advance. Remember, safety is your first consideration. At any stage, you can pair up players and have one toss the ball to his or her partner. A variation of this drill is to have the goalkeeper take two steps to each side and place a marker at each side. The goalkeeper can dive but not step outside these marks. The partner tosses or passes the ball to the outside of each mark, forcing the goalkeeper to dive after the ball.

(7.5) Ball Handling Exercises

Purpose. To practice handling the ball and developing a feel for the ball.

Organization. Provide each player with a ball and position players about 3 yd apart.

Directions. Players handle balls in three different patterns.

- Have players spread their legs about shoulder width apart and move the ball in a figure 8 pattern (see Figure 7-21a).
- Have players spread their legs about shoulder width apart and bounce the ball on the ground around the body by bending the trunk, as shown in Figure 7-21b.
- Have players spread their legs about shoulder width apart and hold the ball between their legs with one hand in front of the legs and one hand behind the legs (see Figure 7-21c). Players try to switch hands from one side of the body to the other, catching the ball before it touches the ground.

Fig. 7-21a

Fig. 7-21b

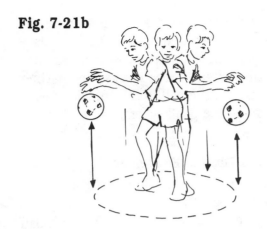

Fig. 7-21c

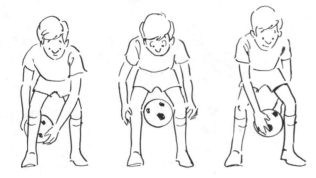

(7.6) Collect and Squeeze

Purpose. To practice collecting and securing shots.

Organization. Pair up players, with one ball per pair. Have each player face his or her partner about 5 to 10 yd apart and position pairs of players down the field with plenty of room separating the pairs. One player is the thrower, and one is the goalkeeper.

Directions. The thrower tries to throw the ball past the goalkeeper, but must throw the ball (a) within two steps to each side and (b) not above hand's reach of the goalkeeper. The goalkeeper tries to collect the ball. The goalkeeper scores one point for each ball he or she catches. The thrower scores one point for each ball the goalkeeper does not catch. Throws outside of the specified limits score one point for the goalkeeper. Switch after every 10 throws. This game can be combined with throw-in practice by requiring players to throw from overhead with both feet on the ground.

(7.7) Think Fast

Purpose. To develop goalkeeper movement and reaction skills.

Organization. Divide your team into groups of at least three players, or practice with goalkeepers separately. Have a good supply of balls. Position the goalkeeper in front of the goal with his or her back toward the shooter. The shooters stand about 20 yd from the goal.

Directions. As the shooter kicks the ball, all other players shout "Shot!" and the direction of the ball, signaling the goalkeeper to turn and stop the shot. Instruct the players to make their shots challenging but not too fast or too far from the goalkeeper. Rotate positions after each shot.

(7.8) Throw and Punt

Purpose. To practice throwing and punting from the goal area.

Organization. Divide the team in half and position the two groups at opposite ends of the field. Divide each group in half, with two goalkeepers and two lines of receivers. Supply each receiver with a ball.

Directions. Practice each throwing and punting technique, progressing from bowling the ball to players close to the goal, to punting the ball to players near midfield. Players rotate from goalkeeper to receiver after at least three passes with each technique. This drill can also be used with one goalkeeper while the team is practicing how to initiate an offense or playing small-sided minigames.

Part II: Soccer Tactics

Keeping possession of the ball through ball control is really the key to playing soccer. Individual players need to develop their soccer skills so they can control the ball by receiving, dribbling, passing, heading, and shooting. Ball control is important for offense, because your team could not score goals if they could not control the ball. Ball control is also important for defense, because the longer your team controls the ball, the less time your opponent will have the ball and be able to attack your goal.

This part of the book presents how to teach players to work as a team to control the ball. Included in this section are principles of organizing a team, positional play, offensive and defensive tactics, and set plays. Because teamwork is complicated and requires practice in gamelike settings, minigames and practice activities that stress playing under pressure of defenders are presented for you. You will find that practicing under gamelike settings really helps your players develop their skills, enjoy playing soccer, and play well in actual games.

Chapter 8: Systems and Positional Play

Introduction: Organizing the Team

A system of play refers to the formation of the players on the field for each team. For example, a team that plays with four defenders, three midfielders, and three forwards uses a 4–3–3 system of play. Explain to your players that soccer rules do not specify where players must be positioned. Instead, playing systems should be designed to take advantage of the skills of each player on a team. Some systems emphasize offense, some defense, and others are balanced playing systems. Therefore, in order to coach your players effectively, you need to become familiar with and teach your players the following topics presented in this chapter:

- Understanding Offensive and Defensive Functions
- Playing Positions and Responsibilities
- Playing Systems
- Teaching Progression for Systems and Positional Play
- Games and Activities for Systems and Positional Play

Understanding Offensive and Defensive Functions

Because ball possession changes so often during games, young players may be confused about when their team is on offense and when it is on defense. Tell your players that whenever their team has control of the ball, they are on offense; whenever the other team has the ball, they are on defense. This is true whether they play a position that is primarily defensive in nature, such as defender, or a position that is primarily offensive in nature, such as forward.

Offensive Functions

Your team has two primary functions when on offense. The first function is to keep possession by controlling the ball. The second function is to attack the opponents' goal by advancing the ball. Explain that controlling the ball is the result of good passing and teamwork, of working together to keep the ball away from the opponents. If players work together to control the ball, they will have many opportunities to score. It is important to teach these two offensive playing functions because soccer is so quick. For example, your team could be playing defense and stop a shot or intercept a pass near your goal. Your team would now be on offense with the primary responsibility of your players shifting to controlling the ball and moving it away from the goal. If your team has the ball near midfield, protecting the goal is not so important, and the function of the offense should shift to advancing the ball and attacking the opponents' goal.

Defensive Functions

Your team also has two primary functions when on defense. The first function is to prevent the offensive team from advancing. The second function is to defend the goal from the attacking team. Following the example above, if your team loses the ball while attacking the opponents' goal, your team is now on defense and should attempt to delay the opposing team and try to steal the ball. If the opposing team is attacking your goal, the emphasis would no longer be simply on preventing the offense from advancing downfield, but would be on protecting the goal.

Communication and Teamwork

Whatever playing system your team uses, the ultimate success will depend upon (a) positioning your players where they will be most effective, (b) communication among players, and (c) teamwork among players. Player positions and responsibilities are presented later in this chapter. For now, let's examine communication and teamwork.

Good communication among players must be emphasized at each practice session. Teach your players to communicate both *verbally*, using short and specific words or phrases, and *nonverbally*, using clear movements or gestures. For example, teach players who are open for a pass from teammates to call for the ball or to move into a position to receive a ball and point to where it should be passed. Teach players who want to pass to teammates to call out the player's name and to point to him or her. Also, teach players, when they are guarding an attacking player with the ball, to point to other players who need to be marked by teammates.

Teammates can also help each other by calling out situations that another does not see. For example, teach players to alert teammates when an offensive player or defensive player sneaks up from behind to create an offensive advantage or to try to steal the ball. Teamwork involves more than communication. You will need to encourage your players to hustle; to move, when not in possession of the ball, to open areas; and to provide support after losing possession, poor passes, or scored goals. Set an example by rewarding

hustle and effort and by offering constructive advice rather than blaming players for mistakes.

Coaching Points for Understanding Offensive and Defensive Functions

1. Players on offense have the two functions of keeping possession by controlling the ball and of attacking the opponents' goal by advancing the ball.
2. Players on defense have the two functions of hindering the offensive team and of defending the goal from the attacking team.
3. Develop short, clear verbal and nonverbal cues, and practice these at every practice session.
4. Positively encourage players' hustle and effort.

Playing Positions and Responsibilities

After your players understand the general functions of offensive and defensive play, they will be ready to learn the playing areas and responsibilities for specific positions. Explain that over many years three basic playing positions have developed for effective soccer play: (a) defenders, (b) midfielders, and (c) forwards (see Figure 8-1).

Fig. 8-1

Defenders

Defenders or fullbacks are the players who most often play near their own goal (see Figure 8-2).

The primary responsibility of defenders is to protect the goal, but they must also be able to initiate the offense from near the goal after a shot is stopped or after a goal kick. Effective defenders possess the following abilities:

- Quickness and speed to counteract quick forwards
- Good tackling skills
- Determination and aggressiveness
- Good heading skills (for older players)

Fig. 8-2

Defenders can be assigned slightly different functions depending upon the exact playing system used. Defenders near the side of the field are called *wing fullbacks*. Defenders near the center of the field are called *center fullbacks*. Defenders called *sweepers* play in the center and are the closest defensive players to the goal. *Stoppers* play in the center but further from the goal and often are the first defenders to challenge attackers.

Midfielders

Midfielders play the middle of the soccer field between the defenders and the forwards (see Figure 8-3). These players are real workhorses, because they roam wide to help forwards attack when on offense and to help defenders protect the goal when on defense. Therefore, midfielders should possess the following abilities:

- Good dribbling skills
- Good stamina and endurance
- Good ball control
- Good anticipation of plays

Fig. 8-3

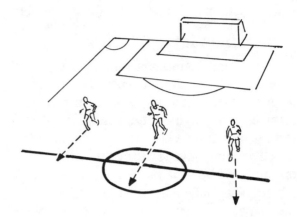

Midfielders can also be assigned different functions depending upon the playing system used. *Outside midfielders* play near the sides of the field, and *center midfielders* play in the center area of the field.

Forwards

Forwards or strikers play nearest the opponents' goal (see Figure 8-4). Because they are your team's primary attackers, the defensive team will try to outnumber the forwards to counter any attack. This means that in order to attack the goal effectively, forwards should possess the following abilities:

- Good dribbling skills
- Good passing skills
- Movement when not in possession of the ball
- Good heading skills
- Good running speed and quick feet

Fig. 8-4

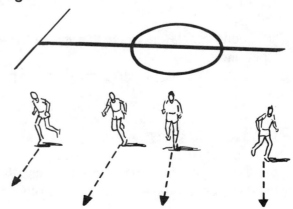

Forwards can be classified as *wingers*, who play near the side of the field, and as *center forwards*, who play near the middle of the field.

Determine Playing Positions

With a young team consisting of players with different abilities, and with special rules for some leagues that require all players on a roster to receive equal playing time, you will need to determine carefully where to position players for effective team play. Try to evaluate the abilities of your players and place them at a position where they will benefit individually and contribute to the team. Strategically positioning players to take advantage of their strengths and to limit the disadvantages of their weaknesses will help provide a more balanced team and will help weak and insecure players from developing a fear of failure.

However, avoid limiting players to only one position. Encourage them to practice playing each position and to select two positions they would like to play each game. Always evaluate the progress of each player and challenge him or her to develop his or her skills in low pressure situations, such as scrimmage games during practices.

Coaching Points for Playing Positions and Responsibilities

1. Defenders play near their own goal, and their primary responsibility is protecting the goal.
2. Midfielders control the middle of the field and play both offense and defense.
3. Forwards play nearest the opponents' goal, and their primary responsibility is playing offense.
4. Position your players where they can exercise their strengths.
5. Encourage players to play more than one position.

Playing Systems

A *playing system* is the term used to describe how players are positioned and consequently determines whether a team emphasizes offensive play or defensive play. Playing systems are referred to according to the respective number of defenders, midfielders, and forwards. For example, a 4–2–4 system positions four defenders, two midfielders, and four forwards on a team (see Figure 8-5).

Fig. 8-5

Find the Best System for Your Team

Most coaches feel that four defensive players are essential to play effective defense. However, there is room for flexibility in establishing the ratios of midfielders to forwards.

Systems that position more forwards than midfielders tend to emphasize offensive play (see Figure 8-6); systems that position more midfielders than forwards tend to emphasize a more defensive approach (see Figure 8-7); and systems that position equal numbers of forwards and midfielders tend to emphasize a balance of offensive and defensive play as shown in Figure 8-8.

Fig. 8-6

Fig. 8-7

Fig. 8-8

In recent years the 4–2–4, 4–3–3, and 4–4–2 systems have been quite popular for high level soccer teams. Because your team will be composed largely of young, inexperienced players, however, you will need to experiment to find the system that is best for your team. Also, many leagues for players under age 12 play "short sided," or with fewer than 11 players. For such leagues, you will need to adjust the number of defenders, midfielders, and forwards in your playing system. The general principles, however, for emphasizing offensive or defensive play will help you design a system just right for your team.

Remember to be flexible when choosing your system. Nothing is etched in stone, so be prepared to experiment with different formations if things do not go well. The best chemistry may take a while to develop, and you may need to make many positional changes with some players. Look for changes in the development of your players and never stereotype them for certain roles. You may be pleasantly surprised with some changes you never thought would work.

System Flexibility

Two dangers await you when first using a playing system. First, the nice, neat system you thought would work is now chaotic because your players are running helter-skelter around the field. Second, in their zeal to maintain a playing system, players may be reluctant to move out of a perfectly aligned 4–3–3 system to where they need to play. In either case mentioned above, the playing system is ineffective. An important aspect of each system is allowing flexibility for players to shift positions in relation to the ball or to opponents, when necessary.

To avoid a breakdown in the playing system your team chooses to use, explain that the system should be played flexibly. For example, as shown in Figure 8-9, defenders who need to move to the middle of the field to help midfielders should do so while the other defenders shift to help play the area vacated. Playing positional scrimmage games (8.2) will help you instruct players on how to adjust their playing positions.

Fig. 8-9

Similarly, midfielders can move with forwards to attack the goal, and forwards can shift deep to their own half to protect the goal. After players are no longer needed in other areas, they can return to the more structured playing system. The guiding principle for system flexibility is to *provide support to either advance the ball or to protect the goal.*

Coaching Points for Playing Systems

1. Playing systems should place the number of defenders, midfielders, and forwards where your players can be most effective.
2. Generally most teams play with four defensive players. Systems emphasizing offensive play use more forwards than midfielders. Systems emphasizing defensive play use more midfielders than forwards. Systems emphasizing a balance use equal numbers of forwards and midfielders.
3. Allow your players to help decide the playing system.
4. Playing systems should be flexible to provide support to either advance the ball or to protect the goal.

Teaching Progression for Systems and Positional Play

1. Teach players the two functions and objectives of offensive play: keeping possession by controlling the ball and attacking the opponents' goal by advancing the ball.
2. Teach players the two functions and objectives of defensive play: preventing the offense from advancing and protecting the goal.
3. Teach players how to communicate with each other and emphasize it during every practice session.
4. Teach players the playing positions and responsibilities of defenders, midfielders, and forwards.
5. Teach players the principles of offensive, defensive, and balanced playing systems. Allow players to help select a playing system that is effective for them.
6. Teach players how to play each system flexibly, allowing for support in advancing the ball and for protecting the goal.

Games and Activities for Systems and Positional Play

(8.1) Positional Scrimmage Games

Purpose. To practice positional play and responsibilities.

Organization. Play regular full-sided or small-sided scrimmage games.

Directions. Use scrimmage games to direct players' positioning for different situations. For example, if the ball is taken to the opponents' goal area, instruct the midfielders and defenders to advance an appropriate distance (see Figure 8-10). If the ball is taken to the left side of the field, instruct players to shift to the left side, directing defensive strength at the ball (see Figure 8-11).

Fig. 8-10

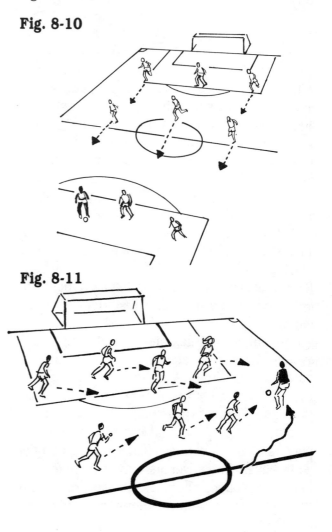

Fig. 8-11

Chapter 9: Offensive Tactics

Introduction: Creating Goals

One reason why soccer has not captured the attention of some American spectators is that the number of goals scored in a game is relatively low when compared to the points scored in sports like basketball and football. One reason few goals are scored is that many coaches emphasize defense instead of offense. This indicates a basic truth that young soccer players often fail to understand: *goals do not happen, they are created*. Sometimes a player just seems to be at the right place at the right time, or a goalkeeper misplays a shot, or a ball ricochets off a player into the goal. Such plays do occur, but they seldom happen, and they occur because a good shot was created, or the right player did move to the right place at the right time. Without players actively creating scoring situations, your team will seldom score.

Many offensive tactics have been developed throughout the period of more than one hundred years that formal soccer has been played. To help your team benefit from them and learn to create goal-scoring opportunities, the following topics are presented:

• Offensive Principles
• Teaching Progression for Offensive Tactics
• Games and Activities for Offensive Tactics

Offensive Principles

The following principles are the basis for effective offensive ball movement and attack. Similar to the basic playing system principle of providing support to advance the ball, these principles will help your players understand how to create scoring opportunities. Your players should try to *attack as often as possible*. Ball possession changes often in soccer, and your players should take advantage of every opportunity that these changes present. Your players will need to *spread out the attack* to create space and to create goal-scoring opportunities. If players *attack with depth* to support teammates and to penetrate toward the goal, they will be able to create space and provide many play options. One way to create space is to *move, with or without possession of the ball*, eluding defenders and moving to open areas. Players must also know how to exploit a *one-on-one situation* to beat defenders and create space for other teammates. *Passing the ball from the side of the field into the area in front of the goal* is an effective method for passing the ball into this area when teammates have created space. Passing the ball from the center of the field into this area is also effective. The Scoring Pattern Drill (9.1) will help your players learn and practice these offensive principles.

Attack the opponents' goal as often as possible. This does not mean, however, that players should shoot haphazardly from midfield. Explain that shots are only effective when realistic scoring options are created and that when they are created, players should not hesitate to shoot. Also, passes and shots often bounce or roll around in front of a goal. Explain that players should often follow the ball and shoot free balls in front of the goal.

Spread Out the Attack

Spreading out the attack accomplishes two objectives: (a) your players have more room to pass, shoot, and dribble and (b) the defense cannot effectively guard against a spread-out formation as easily as against a more compact formation. Young players tend to only make runs toward the goal to receive passes (see Figure 9-1). But this leaves little room behind the defense to pass the ball without it being intercepted, and if defenders follow the players into this area, the goal is more easily defended. Rather than having your players run directly toward the goal, instruct them to run diagonally away from the goal (see Figure 9-2), creating space behind the defense for other teammates to receive passes and to shoot. Useful activities to teach and practice creating space by spreading out the attack are Creating Space Away From the Goal (9.2) and Creating Space Close to the Goal (9.3).

Fig. 9-1

Fig. 9-2

Attack With Depth

The defensive team can guard against a spread-out attack if the attack is in a straight line (see Figure 9-3), because the defensive team knows that players will simply pass across the field to each other. Consequently, teach your players to *attack with depth* or support teammates, as shown in Figure 9-4. Demonstrate how players can provide depth by playing in front of and behind the ball. With depth the ball can be passed toward the goal for shots or back to teammates to set up another play. Use the Give-and-Go or Wall Pass (9.4), Two Versus One Overlap (9.5), and Three Versus One Overlap (9.6) to practice attacking with depth.

Fig. 9-3

Fig. 9-4

Move With and Without Possession of the Ball

Often players fail to understand the importance of moving into position while someone else has the ball, causing many players to be less effective than they could be. Instruct your players to *move with and without possession of the ball* into open areas from which they can pass, shoot, or dribble. Most often it is the players without the ball who are instrumental in creating goals, because they actually create the play by being in the right place at the right time to receive a pass and to shoot at the goal.

Exploiting the One-on-One Situation

If your opponents are well organized defensively, reducing your team's ability to create space, your players can dribble past defensive players to create space. When defenders are beaten by dribbling around them, other defenders are forced to leave their positions to challenge the dribbler, creating space for teammates to move into position to receive passes and to shoot (see Figure 9-5).

Fig. 9-5

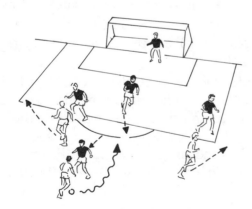

Of course, as the player with the ball dribbles around opponents, teammates must use the other offensive principles to create space and to support the dribbler. Instruct players to move at diagonals and away from the dribbler, taking other defenders away from him or her. If teammates move toward the dribbler, defenders will follow, and it is difficult for a dribbler to beat several defenders in succession. Exploiting the

one-on-one situation can be developed by practicing Beat the Defender (9.7), Run Around (9.8), and Two Versus Two Dribble (9.9).

Pass the Ball From the Side Into the Area in Front of the Goal

Because the most direct shooting angles are from the center of the field, an attack directly from the center of the field seems quite logical. But one factor usually prevents this. Most often, several defenders closely cover the area in front of their own goal, blocking these good shooting angles and forcing the ball to the side into less effective shooting angles. Consequently, in order to attack the goal effectively when along the side of the goal area, teach your players to *pass the ball from the side into the area in front of the goal* where they can shoot more directly at the goal (see Figure 9-6). An important component of this principle is to pass the ball from near the goal line into the goalmouth so that the ball is out of the goalkeeper's reach. Sometimes a goalkeeper will move out of the goal area to chase a ball just out of his or her reach, leaving the goal open. Creating Space Close to the Goal (9.3) provides useful activities for teaching and practicing this principle.

Fig. 9-6

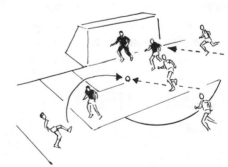

Coaching Points for Offensive Principles

1. Always try to create a numerical advantage or to create an open area from which a player can dribble, shoot, or receive passes.

2. Spread out the attack to create space.
3. Attack with depth or provide support for the attack by playing in front of and behind the ball.
4. Dribble past defenders when other options are not possible. This will advance the ball and help create other passing and shooting options for teammates.
5. If forced to the side of the area in front of the goal, pass the ball from the side into the goal-mouth setting up shots from more direct angles.

Teaching Progression for Offensive Tactics

1. Teach players that goals do not just happen; goals are created.
2. Teach players to attack with depth, providing support in front of and behind the ball.
3. Teach players how to spread out the attack to create open spaces by drawing defenders away from an area and by moving to areas free of defenders.
4. Teach players to be mobile, moving with and without possession of the ball.
5. Teach players to exploit the one-on-one situation and to beat defenders by dribbling.
6. Teach players that, when forced to the side, they should pass the ball into the goal area, out of the goalkeeper's reach.

Games and Activities for Offensive Tactics

(9.1) Scoring Pattern

Purpose. To practice offensive tactical principles when attacking the goal.

Organization. Divide the team into groups of four or five players. One player is the goalkeeper, and the other players are the attackers; there are no defenders. Use one ball per group. Play on a regulation field or in grids 20 by 20 yd.

Directions. Attackers move the ball from outside the penalty area toward the area in front of the goal to score goals. With each sequence they should try to implement principles of offensive attacks (spread out the attack, attack with depth, move with and without possession of the ball, and pass from the side into the goal area). You can instruct your players to emphasize just one principle each sequence or several principles at once. After your players have demonstrated that they understand how to apply these principles and can adequately control the ball, include one or two defenders. Rotate players from goalkeeper to attackers, to defenders (when used), after every three sequences.

Activities for Creating Space

The following activities have been designed to practice creating space away from and between defenders and to create passing and goal-scoring opportunities. The exercises focus on how to create space away from the goal and in front of the goal.

(9.2) Creating Space Away From the Goal

Purpose. To practice eluding defensive players and creating space to receive passes or to free a teammate.

Organization. This exercise can be played with any number of players, but offensive players should outnumber defensive players. In this exercise, three offensive players are opposed by two defenders and one goalkeeper. Position players, as shown in Figure 9-7, in an area 30 by 30 yd with a goal area at one end, with one ball per group.

Directions. Instruct the players who are without possession of the ball to run wide and toward the ball, creating space to receive passes and, if defenders follow them, creating an open area down the middle where the player with possession of the ball can dribble. Keep passing and moving to create space by moving to support the ball and to create passing or dribbling lanes to advance the ball toward the goal. Score one point for each goal and one point for each time the ball is intercepted or kicked out of the grid. Alternate offense and defense after one team scores five points.

Fig. 9-7

(9.3) Creating Space Close to the Goal

Purpose. To practice offensive movements for creating goal-scoring opportunities near the goal.

Organization. Divide the team into groups of seven players. Four players are on offense, two are on defense, and one plays goalkeeper. Play in front of the goal on a regulation field or on a 30 by 30-yd grid with a goal area marked at one end of the grid.

Directions. Design a scoring situation for your players to create, and specify for the offensive players how they should move to execute the play. The objective is to create space in the area directly in front of the goal (see Figure 9-8). Defensive players should try to prevent the play. Two examples for you to use follow.

Fig. 9-8

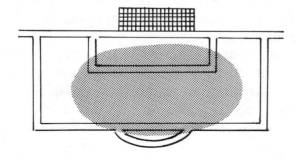

Far Post Attack

As shown in Figure 9-9, this play is designed to create space near the goal area that is farthest from where the ball is passed. The play begins with offensive player O1 passing the ball from near the center of the field toward the side to offensive player O3, who dribbles toward the goal line. As he or she dribbles toward the goal line, offensive players O1 and O2 run into the goal area toward the near post, drawing defenders X1 and X2 with them and creating space for offensive player O4 at the far post. When near the goal line, offensive player O3 passes, on the ground or in the air, to the far post area. Offensive player O4 should time his or her run to this area to try and receive the pass just as it arrives, then shoot or head at goal.

Fig. 9-9

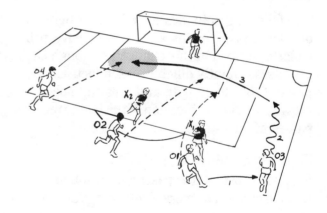

Near Post Attack

As shown in Figure 9-10, attacking the near post is similar to attacking the far post. In this situation, offensive players O4 and O2 are marked by defensive players X1 and X2. The play begins with offensive player O1 passing from near the center toward the side to offensive player O3, who dribbles toward the goal line. Offensive players O4 and O2 run toward the far post area, drawing the defenders with them and creating space at the near post area. When near the goal line, offensive player O3 passes on the ground to offensive player O1, who times his or her run to meet the ball, then shoots at the goal.

Fig. 9-10

Activities to Practice Passing and Moving

The following activities have been designed to develop passing skills and the offensive principles described in this chapter. Although each exercise is slightly different, each focuses upon passing to a teammate and creating space by moving without possession of the ball to receive passes and to shoot.

(9.4) Give-and-Go or Wall Pass 2

Purpose. To practice passing and moving forward to create a numerical advantage and space to pass or shoot.

Organization. Play in a 20- by 20-yd grid or in the goal area 20 or 30 yd in front of the goal. Place a set of cones as goal, or use the actual goal. Position players as shown in Figure 9-11, with one attacker, one player acting as a wall, one defender, and one goalkeeper. Position the wall player at a diagonal about 10 yd from the attacker and the defender 10 yd directly in front of the attacker. Divide the team into as many groups as possible to keep players active.

Directions. Attackers are confronted by the defender and pass to the receiver. As soon as he

or she passes, the attacker runs around the defender toward the goal to receive a return pass from the receiver/passer. If the pass is good, the attacker can shoot at the goal. Rotate playing positions after each attempt.

Fig. 9-11

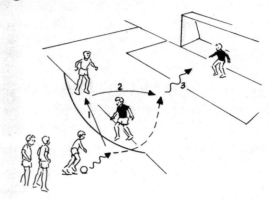

(9.5) Two Versus One Overlap

Purpose. To practice passing and moving to advance the ball.

Organization. Position players as shown in Figure 9-12, with one attacker, one receiver/passer, one defender, and one goalkeeper. In this exercise the defender plays behind the receiver/passer, and the attacker begins 10 to 15 yd from the receiver/passer. Play in a 20- by 20-yd grid and mark a goal area at the back of the grid, or play in the goal area 20 to 30 yd from the goal.

Directions. The attacker passes to the receiver, who is challenged from behind by the defender. After passing, the attacker runs around the receiver and defender, and the receiver then passes the ball on toward the goal to the attacker. If the pass is good, the attacker can shoot at the goal. The key to this practice is for the receiver to turn and face the defender. If the receiver cannot turn, then the attacker should stay back to support the receiver rather than overlap. Rotate player positions after each attempt. For highly skilled players, add an extra defender to mark the attacker.

Fig. 9-12

(9.6) Three Versus One Overlap

Purpose. To practice passing and moving to advance the ball.

Organization. Position players as shown in Figure 9-13, with two attackers (O1 and O2), one receiver (O3), one defender, and one goalkeeper. In this exercise, the defender plays behind the receiver, and the two attackers play at diagonals about 10 yd from the receiver. Play in a 20- by 20-yd grid and mark a goal area at the back of the grid, or play in the goal area 20 to 30 yd from the goal.

Directions. The attacker with the ball (O1) passes to the receiver (O3) and runs around toward the goal. The receiver passes the ball out to the other attacker (O2) providing support, who then passes to the attacker running toward the goal. This can be varied to begin from either side with either attacker. Rotate positions after each turn. For highly skilled players, add an extra defender to mark the attackers.

Fig. 9-13

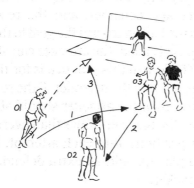

Activities for One-on-One Play

The following activities are designed to practice exploiting the one-on-one situation and applying the other offensive principles to do so. We recommend that you practice the following activities in order, progressing from basic one-on-one play to more advanced two versus one and two versus two play.

(9.7) Beat the Defender

Purpose. To practice dribbling past a defender one-on-one.

Organization. Divide the team into groups of two players, with one ball per group. One player is the offensive player, the other is the defender. Position players in a 20- by 20-yd or 30- by 20-yd grid, as shown in Figure 9-14.

Directions. The defensive player begins play by standing at least 10 yd from the offensive player and passing the ball to him or her. The offensive player tries to dribble past the defender to the end of the area without going out to the side of the playing area or losing the ball. The defender tries to intercept the ball or kick it out of the playing area. Rotate positions after every three tries.

Fig. 9-14

(9.8) Run Around

Purpose. To practice dribbling past a defender, moving with and without possession of the ball, and providing support.

Organization. Divide the team into groups of three players, with one ball per group. Two players are on offense, and one is on defense.

Position players in a 30- by 20-yd grid, as shown in Figure 9-15.

Directions. The defensive player begins play by standing at least 10 yd from the offensive players and passing the ball. Offensive players try to advance the ball by making wall passes, overlapping passes, and dribbling past the defender. Switch positions after the ball has been dribbled past the end of the playing area, or after the defender has stolen the ball or kicked it out of the playing area.

Fig. 9-15

(9.9) Two Versus Two Dribble

Purpose. To practice moving with and without possession of the ball, providing support, and dribbling past a defender.

Organization. Divide the team into groups of four players, with two offensive players and two defenders. Position players, as shown in Figure 9-16, in a 30- by 30-yd area with a goal marked at one end, or play on a regulation field in front of the goal. Use one ball per group.

Directions. Play begins with the defensive players standing at least 10 yd from the offensive players and passing the ball to them. Once the ball is passed, the defensive players can challenge the ball. The offensive players try to create space to dribble one-on-one to the goal area, or pass to create a shooting opportunity. Encourage players to use the fundamental playing principles, presented in chapters 2 and 8, and principles of effective offensive play, presented in this chapter. Award one point for each goal scored. Explain that if the offensive player without the ball does not draw the defender marking him or her away from the ball, the offensive player with the ball will have two defenders to beat rather than one. A good way to keep defenders from double teaming the player with the ball is to award one point each time the offensive players complete three consecutive passes. This forces one defender to mark each offensive player.

Fig. 9-16

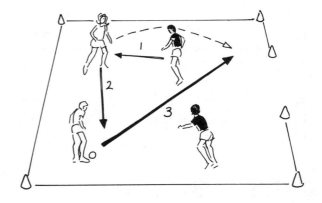

Chapter 10: Defensive Tactics

Introduction: Do Not Forget the Defense

Because scoring is glamorous, many young players want to play as forwards while few volunteer to play as defenders. In reality, defenders are at least equal in importance to forwards and often provide a springboard for a team's offense. Playing defense is also a difficult part of soccer, because players must react to the movement of the opposing team and, if not careful, can easily be caught a step behind the players they cover. Teaching your players the following topics will help them effectively defend the goal, regain possession of the ball, and launch into the offense:

- Defensive Principles
- Defensive Skills
- Implementing the Defense
- Teaching Progression for Defensive Tactics
- Games and Activities for Defensive Tactics

Defensive Principles

Just as principles have developed to guide offensive tactics, so too have principles developed to guide defensive tactics. In fact, many of these team defensive principles have been designed to counteract those offensive principles discussed in chapter 9. This constant struggle between the offense and the defense, with each trying to outsmart and outplay the other, is one reason soccer is such a popular game. To effectively defend against the opponents' offense, your team will need to learn how to (a) mark or guard offensive players between the opponent and the goal, (b) delay the offense, (c) force the ball away from the goal, (d) reduce the passing and shooting angles, (e) adjust the defensive alignment, and (f) defend with depth. In addition to the games and activities listed in chapter 9, Offensive Tactics, Defending in Possession Keep-Away (10.1), Defending From Behind (10.2), and Preventing the Through Pass (10.3) will help your players learn and apply these defensive principles.

Mark or Guard Players Between the Opponent and the Goal

The first individual defensive principle to teach your players is to *mark or guard players by positioning themselves between the opponent and the goal* (see Figure 10-1). Show your players how this will prevent the opponent from running past them and gaining an offensive advantage.

Fig. 10-1

The distance between the defender and opponent depends upon how far the current play is from the goal. Explain that the further from the goal an offensive player is positioned, the less tightly defenders should play the opponent (see Figure 10-2). Players need not closely mark an opponent near midfield, because scoring is not a threat, and because defenders can use the space between them and the goal to react to player movement. However, if defenders closely mark an opponent far from the goal and the opponent beats the defender, then the defender has a long distance to run and will probably not catch the opponent.

Fig. 10-2

Delay the Offense

The second individual defensive principle to teach your players is to *delay the offense*. Delaying the offense is important, because the more time the offense takes to create plays, the more time the defense has to react to the plays. This principle is particularly applicable when teams change possession of the ball. For example, if your team is attacking the opponents' goal and the ball is intercepted, then players nearest the ball should challenge the player with the ball, delaying the offense deep in their territory and allowing the rest of your team time to move into defensive position (see Figure 10-3). Of course, this is more important when the ball is lost in your team's half of the field. If the ball is lost in the middle of the field, delaying the offense may mean retreating a few steps to stay between the attacker and the goal, reducing dribbling and passing options toward the goal.

Fig. 10-3

Direct the Ball Away From the Goal

The third individual defensive principle to teach your players is to force your opponents to *play the ball away from the goal* (see Figure 10-4). Tell players that it is more difficult to score from the side of the goal than from in front of the goal, therefore they should try to deny offensive players the inside of the field and force the ball to the outside. Playing position is the key for doing this. Demonstrate how playing behind and slightly to the inside of their opponent enables them to react to moves inside and toward the goal.

Fig. 10-4

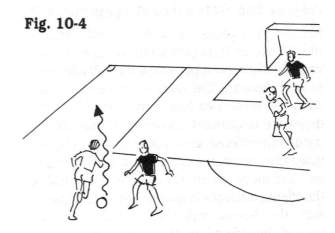

Reduce the Passing and Shooting Angle

Playing an opponent one-on-one is quite a challenge for any soccer player, especially for a young one. When playing one-on-one, particularly when close to the goal, your players should stay within two or three steps of the opponent, be ready to react to any moves, and *reduce the passing and shooting angle* (see Figure 10-5).

Fig. 10-5

Explain to your players that moving close to the opposing offensive player effectively reduces the area through which he or she can pass or shoot. This often confuses and frustrates the opponent and results in a turnover to the defending team.

Adjust the Defensive Alignment

Remind your players that the two functions of the defense are (a) to prevent the offense from advancing, then attempt to steal the ball and (b) to protect the goal. The most effective way to accomplish these two functions is to *adjust the defensive alignment* according to the offense used. If the offense attempts to advance the ball down the middle, the defense will need to "tighten" and move toward the middle of the field. If the offense attempts to advance the ball along the side, the defense will need to shift and play toward the side where the ball is controlled.

The general method for varying the defensive alignment is to always cover the area most vulnerable to attack, shifting other players to concentrate on stopping the ball (see Figure 10-6). This provides balance across the field. Notice that the shaded area in Figure 10-6 indicates the area of the field from which high percentage shots can be taken.

Fig. 10-6

As the ball is advanced near to the goal, players should funnel toward the goal area (see Figure 10-7). This makes crossing the ball in front of the goal more difficult. Also, because outside shots are from such a poor angle, most teams will prefer to control the ball to the side rather than take a poor shot.

Fig. 10-7

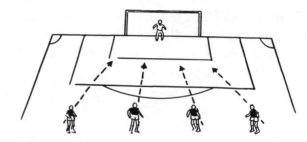

Defend With Depth

Just as the offense will attack with depth, so too should your team *defend with depth*. As shown in Figure 10-8, demonstrate how to provide defensive support by playing behind the primary defender or line of defenders. Playing straight across the field does not provide depth, and offensive players can penetrate such a straight-across defensive line. Defending with depth is the principle used to position one defender as a sweeper in front of the goal and behind other defenders.

Fig. 10-8

Coaching Points for Defensive Principles

1. Play between offensive players and the goal.
2. Deny the inside of the field to offensive players who are in possession of the ball and force opponents to play the ball to the side.
3. Reduce the passing and shooting angle by moving toward the ball and challenging the offensive player when he or she pauses to pass or shoot.
4. Adjust the defensive alignment according to how the offense advances the ball.
5. Always cover the most vulnerable area in front of the goal and shift other players to concentrate on the ball.
6. Provide defensive support to teammates by defending with depth or behind the initial defensive players.
7. If the ball is lost to the opposing team, delay the offense and allow the defense time to set up by challenging the player with the ball.

Defensive Skills

Your players must think defensively when the ball is lost to the opposing team. Therefore, teach defensive skills to every player on the team, not just to those players whose roles are primarily defensive. Forwards and midfielders need to learn defensive skills just as do defenders. The following individual skills specific to defense will help your players become more effective at applying the defensive principles in competitive situations:

• Determining approach angle and speed
• Using an effective stance
• Tackling to win the ball

To practice these defensive skills we recommend you play Small-Sided Scrimmage Games (10.4), Partner Tackle Practice (10.6), and Block Tackle Drill (10.7).

Determining Approach Angle and Speed

The *line of approach*, when challenging an opponent with the ball, is determined by the position of the player on the field and by the proximity of the ball to either goal. In general, instruct players to force the ball away from the goal when playing near their own goal. This follows the defensive principle: *force the ball away from the goal*. As shown in Figure 10-9, if the ball is in the left side of the field, force it further to the left. If the ball is in the right side of the field, force it further to the right. This is especially important if the ball is near your team's goal.

Fig. 10-9

If your team has lost the ball near the opponents' goal, follow the offensive principle: *attack as often as possible*, and the defensive principle: *delay the offense* by approaching the ball to force it toward the opponents' goal, which could lead to a goal-scoring opportunity.

Explain that because the object is to defend against opponents advancing the ball, players should always approach an opponent with the ball as quickly as possible, without hesitating. This does not mean, however, running headlong and out of control. A common problem for players is challenging quickly and without control, rendering them unable to react to countermoves from offensive players. This allows smart offensive players to elude defenders. The defender's main concern is to delay the offense, then to win the ball. Consequently, demonstrate how to (a) approach quickly from a distance,

(b) slow down or stop at a distance where the ball can be played, and (c) if possible, to challenge for the ball.

Using an Effective Stance

When the defender has reached a position where he or she can effectively pressure an opponent in possession of the ball, he or she must adopt the correct stance to maintain defensive pressure. Many players confront opponents square-on with the legs spread from side to side (see Figure 10-10). This is a common mistake that leaves players flat-footed and unable to react to the opponent effectively. Demonstrate how players should stand with the legs spread front to back, facing the direction players want to force the ball, with weight evenly distributed between both feet (see Figure 10-11). This position allows players to turn from side to side or move forward and backward more quickly than a side-to-side stance.

Fig. 10-10

Fig. 10-11

Tackling to Win the Ball

Tackling is a way to challenge players who have possession of the ball in an attempt to win the ball or stop the opponent. The two basic tackling techniques are the *block tackle* and the *slide tackle*. Before teaching these tackling techniques, tell your players that tackling is allowed from the front, side, or rear, as long as players go for the ball and do not touch the player. However, caution your players about tackling from behind. Because the offensive player cannot see behind and the ball is on the other side of the body, tackling from behind can be dangerous. Also, many young players feel they need to tackle often to be good defenders. Though tackling is an important skill, it should be considered as the last resort in an attempt to win the ball from an opponent. Following the correct pressure techniques as outlined above, players should only tackle when they can win the ball and wait to intercept passes or gain possession when a dribbler kicks the ball too far ahead.

Block Tackle

The block tackle, presented in Figure 10-12, looks like an attempt by both players to make an inside-of-the-foot pass. Important points in performing the block tackle are to:

- Be determined to win the ball. Play aggressively.
- Challenge when the ball is away from the player's feet.
- Keep the foot low and try to push the ball over the foot of the opponent or beyond his or her legs.
- Tackle the ball, not the player.

Fig. 10-12

Slide Tackle

If a player with the ball has broken beyond the defense, and the only way to stop the player is to tackle the ball from the side, players may need to use a slide tackle. Slide tackles should be used only as a last resort because (a) the player with the ball could step on or fall on the sliding player, and (b) after sliding, the defender is on the ground and unable to move the ball effectively. The slide tackle is an advanced skill that we suggest be taught only to accomplished players.

We recommend the following progression for teaching players to slide tackle.

1. Practice sliding on grassy areas, preferably wet grass where sliding is easier. If soft, wet grass is not available, make sure that players wear long pants or sweatpants to protect the hips and thighs.
2. Players should begin running and sliding slowly and gradually progress to faster speeds.
3. To slide, players extend the tackling leg with the other knee bent back, sliding on the soft part of the thighs and bottom of the tackling leg (see Figure 10-13).
4. Practice without a ball and, as players become proficient sliders, add a ball without an opponent.
5. After players can tackle a free ball, add an opponent. Begin at walking speed and gradually progress to dribbling at game speed.

Fig. 10-13

Coaching Points for Defensive Skills

1. Approach the opponent at the correct angle to force him or her away from the goal.

2. Approach the opponent at the correct speed to delay the offense and to be able to remain between the opponent and the ball.
3. Use an effective front to back stance.
4. Tackle when possible using the block tackle.
5. Slide tackle only as a last resort.

Implementing the Defense

Now that your players understand the team defensive principles, they need to learn how to implement the principles within an overall defensive system. Two defensive systems or formations used in soccer are (a) man-to-man defense and (b) zone defense. Although these systems specify two distinct methods for playing team defense, the most widely used and successful defenses combine zone and man-to-man marking.

Man-to-Man Defense

Explain that *man-to-man defense* means guarding one player as he or she moves around the field (see Figure 10-14). If playing man-to-man, players should remain close enough to challenge the opponent when he or she pauses to pass or shoot, but far away enough to react to fakes and moves to intercept passes. Also, the closer the ball is to the goal, the closer the defender should play to the opponent. For example, inside the penalty area the defender should play tight defense, but near midfield he or she can play a more loose defense.

Fig. 10-14

Zone Defense

Because attackers often run around the field creating space to dribble, pass, or shoot, the defense can easily become confused by chasing attackers. Explain that defending a certain area or using a *zone defense* solves this problem by assigning each player to defend a particular area or zone of the field. A player marks those attackers who move into his or her zone and does not chase players who move out of the zone.

Zone defenses do have two weaknesses. First, more than one offensive player can enter or *flood* a zone, presenting a numerical advantage for the offense against one defender. As shown in Figure 10-15, when attackers flood a zone, one or more zones are free of attackers, so defenders can shift from these free or open zones into flooded zones and continue to mark attackers. This is particularly useful when playing close to the goal. The secret to this is for defenders not to drift too far from their original zone.

Fig. 10-15

Combine Man-to-Man and Zone Defense

Combining man-to-man and zone defenses provides a flexible and effective defensive system. To combine these systems, instruct your players to play a zone defense outside of the penalty area then switch to a tight man-to-man defense inside the penalty area. Because players are assigned a particular area of the field to play, that is, left midfielder or center fullback, it is easy for young players to understand that they should play man-to-man defense against the opponent assigned to their area of the field.

Coaching Points for Implementing the Defense

1. Man-to-man defense positions one defender against one attacker.
2. Zone defense positions defenders in specific areas or zones. The defender marks an attacker who plays in his or her zone.
3. If attackers leave one or more zones empty to flood another, defenders in the empty zones shift into the flooded zone to help mark attackers.
4. A practical and effective defensive system is a combination of man-to-man and zone. Players play a zone defense until attackers are near the penalty area, then play man-to-man.

Teaching Progression for Defensive Tactics

1. Teach players how to mark or guard opponents between the opponent and the goal.
2. Teach players how to delay the offense.
3. Teach players how to force the ball away from the goal.
4. Teach players how to challenge and reduce the passing and shooting angle.
5. Teach players how to block tackle and, when ready, how to slide tackle.
6. Teach players how to vary the defensive alignment to protect the area in front of the goal and concentrate upon where the ball is played.
7. Teach players to funnel or play a tight defensive alignment near the goal.
8. Teach players to provide depth and support to the defense by playing behind the front line of the defense.
9. Teach players how to play man-to-man and zone defenses, then how to combine man-to-man and zone defenses.

Games and Activities for Defensive Tactics

Defensive tactics can be practiced using many of the games and activities designed for offensive play, simply by placing the emphasis on defensive principles. Therefore, we recommend that you consider using the games and activities presented in chapter 9, Offensive Tactics, to practice defensive tactics. Additionally, other games previously described can be used to practice defensive principles and skills. Circle Keep-Away (2.12) is a fun game to practice approaching the ball and reducing passing angles. Shadowchaser (4.13) will help players mark opponents and assume the correct defensive stance.

(10.1) Defending in Possession Keep-Away

Purpose. To develop defensive skills.

Organization. Divide the team into groups as desired, pairs, 2 versus 1, 3 versus 1, 4 versus 2, etc. The number of offensive players should be equal to or more than the number of defensive players. Position players in an area large enough for the number of players used, with one ball per group.

Directions. The object is for the offensive team to maintain possession of the ball and for the defensive team to steal the ball. Carefully watch the players and stress defensive principles and skills. Encourage defensive players to approach the ball using an effective angle and speed and to reduce passing angles (see Figure 10-16). Possession keep-away games are excellent for observing players and providing hints on how to play defensively. Although this game is presented as part of defensive tactics, offensive tactics can also be practiced using this game. However, we strongly recommend that you stress either defense or offense while this game is played. Stressing both defense and offense could confuse players and hinder rather than stimulate development.

Fig. 10-16

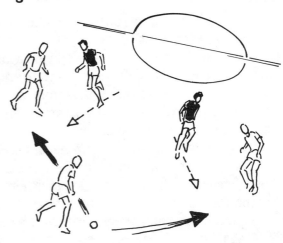

(10.2) Defending From Behind

Purpose. To develop good marking skills and the ability to prevent opponents from turning with the ball.

Organization. Divide the team into groups of three players, with one ball per group. Two players (passer and receiver) are on offense and one player is on defense. Position players in a 10- by 20-yd grid, as shown in Figure 10-17, with two cones placed along the back line as goals.

Directions. The passer passes to the receiver, who stands in the middle of the grid, guarded from behind by the defender. The receiver tries to turn around and dribble or shoot at the goal, while the defender tries to prevent the receiver from turning and dribbling. To prevent the game from dragging on, place a time limit on the game by instructing the passer to count silently to 10 (for highly skilled players) or to 15 (for less skilled players). Score one point for the receiver if he or she hits a goal or one point for the defender if the receiver does not hit a goal. Rotate positions after every attempt. Tell the defender to remain about one arm's length behind the receiver and to follow the receiver to prevent him or her from turning. Stress patience and waiting to win the ball until the receiver tries to turn. Playing this way in games will provide time for the defense to organize more effectively.

Fig. 10-17

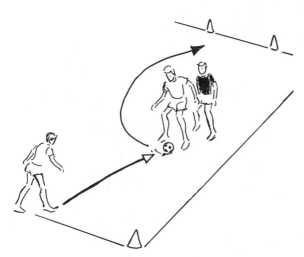

(10.3) Preventing the Through Pass

Purpose. To practice defending against passes.

Organization. Mark an area of three equally spaced zones, as shown below. Divide the team into three groups of two or three players, and position one group in each zone (see Figure 10-18). We recommend using two players for less skilled players and three players for more skilled players.

Directions. The two groups in each end zone are offensive players who try to pass the ball through the middle, defensive zone. Defensive players in this middle zone attempt to block the passes. Players are free to move throughout their zone but cannot move into another zone. Rotate teams after every 3 to 5 minutes.

Fig. 10-18

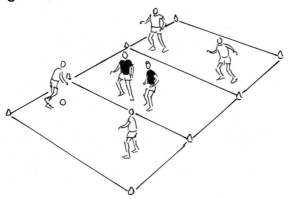

(10.4) Small-Sided Scrimmage Games

Purpose. To practice defensive play in competitive situations.

Organization. Divide the team into equal groups of players as desired, with one ball for every two groups. Position the groups on one half of the soccer field or in playing areas large enough for the groups and with a goal marked at one end.

Directions. Instruct players to play games for a specified time period or until a certain number of points are scored. Options for scoring are to award one point each time (a) the offense scores a goal, (b) each time the defense intercepts the ball, or (c) each time the defense kicks the ball out of play. Observe players and encourage them to apply defensive principles and skills in these competitive situations. As they play, notice trends in individual and team play, and provide specific instructions to guide players to correct mistakes and to emphasize effective play execution.

Variations:

Conditioned Minigames are small-sided games that have special restrictions or limits. Options for small-sided games are:

- No-dribble games where the offense can only pass the ball.
- Mark certain areas of the playing grid, such as two corners, as goal areas. The offensive team must try to pass to a player standing in a goal area (see Figure 10-19).

Fig. 10-19

- Stress moving without possession of the ball and marking players closely by restricting players from receiving a pass from the teammate to whom they just passed.
- Play games with two balls. This makes players concentrate on making a transition from offense to defense, and vice versa, quickly.
- Play games with one ball for every two players (e.g., 5 on 5 with 5 balls). Each time a goal is scored, that ball is dead and cannot be used. Continue until all balls are dead.

(10.5) Marking and Covering Practice

Purpose. To practice implementing defensive principles.

Organization. Divide your team into groups of two to four players, with one ball per two groups. Position two groups in playing grids or in half the soccer field. The larger the number of players the larger the playing area needed.

Directions. Conduct the activity according to the number of players used and the defensive principles emphasized. The three most important defensive principles to emphasize are that (a) the player with the ball is pressured, (b) support is provided by other defenders, and (c) players concentrate in the center of the field in front of the goal. Three options for this activity are:

Two Versus Two Marking and Covering

Two players (O1 and O2) are on offense and two players (D1 and D2) are on defense. Play on a 20- by 30-yd grid with a goal at one end, or play on one half of the soccer field. As shown in Figure 10-20, D1 begins play by passing the ball to O1, and then marks and challenges O1. Because the ball is close to the goal, D2 should play about 5 yd behind and to the side of his or her partner, providing defensive depth. Encourage players to communicate with each other by calling "I have this side marked, Tim!" or "I am covering from behind, Liz!" Two typical situations encountered in games are (a) offensive players passing the ball to each other and the player without possession of the ball moving

to create space (see Figure 10-21) and (b) passing and moving to receive a return pass (see Figure 10-22), such as a wall pass.

Fig. 10-20

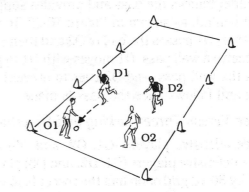

Fig. 10-21

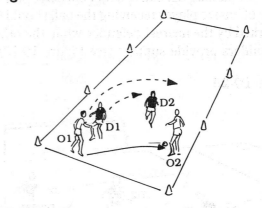

Fig. 10-22

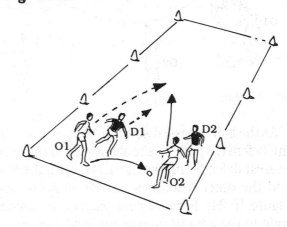

When offensive players pass and move to create space, the role of the defensive players should reverse. For instance, in Figure 10-21, O1 passes to O2, so, D2 should now mark the ball while D1 now provides defensive support.

When offensive players pass and move to receive a return pass, such as a wall pass, one defender must mark the receiver while the other defender follows the pass and provides support from behind, as shown in Figure 10-22. In this instance, O1 passes the ball to O2 and then runs to receive a wall pass. D1 moves with O1 to prevent the wall pass, and D2 tries to prevent the pass and follows once the pass is made.

Three Versus Three Marking and Covering

Three offensive players (O1, O2, and O3) and three defensive players (D1, D2, and D3) play in a 30 by 30-yd grid or on half the soccer field with a goal at one end. One defensive player begins play by passing the ball to either offensive player. The offensive player receiving the ball should be marked by the nearest defender while the other defenders provide support (see Figure 10-23).

Fig. 10-23

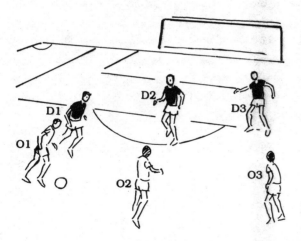

As the ball is passed among offensive players, the defensive players should adjust so that the nearest defender marks the player with the ball and the other defenders provide support (see Figure 10-24). Remind your players to concentrate in the area in front of the goal and not to spread themselves too far apart, leaving one defender isolated in front of the goal to guard the ball.

Fig. 10-24

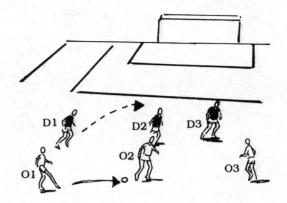

Four Versus Four Marking and Covering

Because many teams will use four defenders, this situation is probably most representative of an actual game situation. The four offensive players (O1, O2, O3, and O4) should be marked by the four defensive players (D1, D2, D3, and D4) in a large playing area or in half the soccer field (see Figure 10-25). Any defensive player can begin by passing the ball to any offensive player. The nearest offensive player should mark the ball while the other defenders provide support.

Fig. 10-25

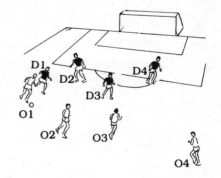

As shown in Figure 10-26, many teams will position one offensive player (O4) wide. Therefore, one defender should be positioned far enough to the side to mark O4 if the ball is passed to him or her, yet close enough to the middle of the field to provide support in front of the goal, if needed.

Fig. 10-26

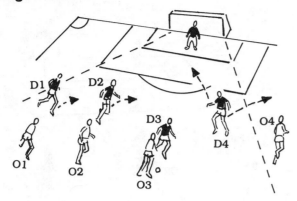

(10.6) Partner Tackle Practice

Purpose. To teach and practice the block tackle.

Organization. Pair up players, and position each pair in a 10- by 10-yd grid, or spread them across the playing field, with one ball per pair.

Directions. One player has the ball and dribbles from one side of the grid toward the other side. The player who is without possession of the ball runs toward the dribbler and challenges for the ball, using a block tackle. The drill should progress gradually through the following three stages, depending upon the skill level and experience of the players.

1. Begin by having the dribbler walk with the ball and not resist the block tackle from the defender.

2. Progress to having the dribbler jog with the ball and try to keep the ball without dribbling around the defender.

3. Progress to having the dribbler try to elude the defender by moving from side to side and backing up but not turning his or her back to the defender.

(10.7) Block Tackle

Purpose. To develop correct tackling skills.

Organization. Divide your team into two groups. Number each player in each group, so that one player from each group is assigned the same number. Align players with the same number opposite each other, about 10 yd apart (see Figure 10-27).

Directions. Instruct players that, when their number is called, they should run toward the ball in front of them and dribble the ball to the opposite side. Each player should try to win the ball by using a block tackle then, dribbling to the opposite side.

Fig. 10-27

Chapter 11: Set Plays

Introduction: Be Prepared

Because soccer is characterized by continuous play, set plays seldom develop during the normal flow of a game. Most set plays develop from *restart situations*, such as throw-ins, goal kicks, direct and indirect free kicks, and corner kicks. Restarts provide offensive and defensive teams the opportunity to position players and to create specific plays. Such set plays are quite effective and account for a large percentage of a team's total goals. Your young athletes will not be capable of remembering and executing many different, complicated plays, so teach your players a few basic set plays from restart situations. As they become more experienced and proficient you can add more challenging plays. Actually, simple plays are usually more effective than complicated plays, because the ball is touched fewer times by fewer players, reducing the risk of error by one of the players, the amount of time needed to execute the play, and the time that defenders have to react to the play.

We suggest you teach set plays in a progression similar to teaching ball control skills.

1. Demonstrate and explain the play.
2. Walk players through the play without a ball, then with a ball.
3. Practice at normal or game speed without opposition, then with opposition.
4. Practice each play in scrimmage games to simulate competitive situations.

The following topics are presented in this chapter to help you teach players set plays:

- Throwing In the Ball
- Plays From Throw-Ins
- Plays From Goal Kicks
- Plays From Indirect and Direct Free Kicks
- Plays From Corner Kicks
- Teaching Progression for Set Plays
- Games and Activities for Set Plays

Of course, your team must also learn to defend against set plays. You cannot assume that other coaches will not teach set plays to their players. For this reason the presentation of each set play includes not only how to execute it but how to defend against it.

Throwing In the Ball

If a ball crosses the sideline out-of-bounds, the team that last touched the ball loses possession, and the opposing team restarts play by *throwing in* the ball. Demonstrate that a proper throw-in begins from behind the head with both hands on the ball and with both feet on the ground (see Figure 11-1). Explain to your players that if they throw in the ball with one hand or raise a foot off the ground, they will lose possession and the other team will be awarded a throw-in.

Fig. 11-1

Players can use three basic techniques to throw in the ball. As shown in Figure 11-1, the first technique is to stand with the feet aligned, about shoulder width apart, swing the ball from behind the head, and release the ball with the arms extended in front of the head. This *standing technique* emphasizes swinging the arms over the head and maintaining balance and should be the first technique taught to young players. It is also the technique used to throw short, accurate passes.

The second technique is to stand with the feet in a front-to-back position (see Figure 11-2). Demonstrate to your players that the thrower holds the ball behind the head and leans back, arching the back and shifting the body weight onto the back leg. To throw the ball, the thrower pushes forward from the rear leg, flexes forward from the stomach, and swings the ball forward. Point out that the rear foot must stay in contact with the ground. This *rocking technique* allows players to throw the ball farther than the standing technique.

Fig. 11-2

The third technique is to stand back from the sideline, run a few steps to gain momentum, and drag the backfoot as the ball is thrown (see Figure 11-3). Such a *run-and-drag technique* allows players to throw the ball longer and with more power than the other two techniques. Teach this advanced technique to players who have mastered the previous two techniques.

Fig. 11-3

Teaching these techniques to your players can be quite a challenge to you as a coach. After all, throwing movements in other sports allow players to throw with one hand and emphasize throwing from one foot. We recommend the following progression to help your players learn throw-ins.

1. Teach players to throw the ball with both hands from behind the head while on their knees. This emphasizes throwing the ball over the head and keeping the body stable and balanced.
2. Teach players to throw short distances while standing up and keeping their feet aligned. Gradually have them progress to throwing longer distances.
3. Teach players to lean back, as they take the ball behind the head, and swing the ball from behind the head to in front of the head, keeping both feet on the ground. After players can do this well, progress from throwing shorter distances to throwing longer distances.
4. Teach players to run and drag their back foot. After players can do this, add swinging the arms over the head without a ball, then add a ball and progress from shorter throw-ins to longer throw-ins.

Plays From Throw-Ins

The role of set plays from throw-ins depends upon the area of the field from which the ball is thrown in. Explain that in the defensive and middle parts of the field, the object is to play safely and to maintain possession of the ball. In the offensive part of the field, the object is to initiate attacks on the opponents' goal.

This means that when players are in the defensive part of the field or close to midfield, they should avoid throwing the ball in the center of the field or too close to their goal. Losing possession in these areas would provide the opposition with prime opportunities to attack quickly. When players are in the offensive part of the field they should try to throw the ball deep toward the goal or to open players who can begin a scoring attack.

Run Away and Cut Back

Your players will probably be guarded closely on throw-ins, so they may have difficulty receiving and controlling the ball unless they elude their defenders. One play for throw-ins is to have the receiving player *run away from the ball and cut back to the ball*, as shown in Figure 11-4. Explain that players should run away toward open areas of the field or toward the goal to draw defenders away from the ball.

Fig. 11-4

By running back toward the ball, players can receive and protect it, keeping the defender behind him or her. If the ball is not thrown while running back, the player can circle away from the thrower, looking for a throw over the defender. A variation of this play is to *run toward the ball and cut away from the ball* toward open areas of the field or toward the goal (see Figure 11-5).

Fig. 11-5

Throw-In and Receive Return Pass

Explain that this play is a variation of the previous two. If a player is guarded closely and cannot receive and control the ball, the thrower can throw, step onto the field, and receive a return pass from the receiver (see Figure 11-6).

Fig. 11-6

Throw-In in the Defensive Part of the Field

Throw-ins taken in the defensive part of the field can lead to easy scoring opportunities for the opponent, unless your players are extremely careful and know how to throw in during these situations. Demonstrate how players can throw the ball down the sideline toward the opponents' goal (see Figure 11-7) as the receiver fakes a run toward the middle of the field and cuts back to the sideline to receive the ball.

Fig. 11-7

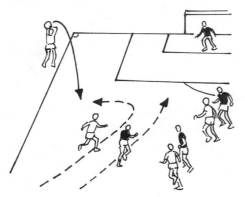

Defense Against Throw-In Plays

To defend against throw-in plays, your players should apply the principles of effective play by remaining between the receiver and the goal. However, if the ball is being thrown in near the goal, or if other teammates are supporting from behind, defensive players can play in front of the receivers, denying them the ball (see Figure 11-8). This also means the ball must be lofted over them.

Fig. 11-8

Coaching Points for Plays From Throw-Ins

1. When in the defensive or midfield areas, protect the ball and goal by making a short throw near the side of the field.
2. When in the offensive areas, attack the goal by throwing toward the opponents' goal and the middle of the field.
3. Elude defenders by running away and cutting back or by running in and cutting away.
4. Protect the ball, when guarded closely, by returning a throw-in to the thrower who steps onto the field.
5. In the defensive part of the field, protect the ball by throwing it down along the sideline toward the opponents' goal.
6. Defend throw-ins near the goal by playing in front of the receiver to deny him or her the ball.

Plays From Goal Kicks

The objectives of a goal kick are (a) to play safe by kicking the ball as far downfield as possible to set up an offensive move or (b) to initiate the offense with a short pass to a teammate. Young players playing on a full-size field may have difficulty clearing the ball beyond the penalty area. If this happens, the ball is often lost to the opposing team directly in front of the goal. To help prevent this, instruct the goalkeeper to kick the ball toward the sideline instead of toward the front of the penalty area, as in Figure 11-9. If your team loses the ball in that area, there is less chance for the opposition to shoot it straight back into your goal.

Fig. 11-9

Short, Control Kicks

For most players, especially young, inexperienced players, short, controlled passes from goal kicks are the best way to initiate the offense. Short kicks from the goal area are easy to receive and control, and easy to advance upfield (see Figure 11-10). If the defense pressures a short kick, the ball can be passed back to the goalkeeper who can make another short pass or boot the ball downfield.

Fig. 11-10

Pass Back to the Goalkeeper

If the defense applies pressure during a goal kick, or if your team wants to kick the ball far downfield quickly, consider passing the ball back to the goalkeeper. Quite simply, the goalkeeper uses the goal kick to pass to a teammate near the penalty area, that teammate returns the ball to the goalkeeper, who can hold it in the hands and punt the ball downfield or can throw it to teammates. Goalkeepers can move to the edge of the penalty area to receive the return pass, preventing defenders from intercepting the ball for an easy shot.

Long, Downfield Kicks

More experienced and mature players can try to kick the ball far downfield to attack the opponents' goal quickly. These goal kicks are difficult to control and often lead to turnovers. We recommend that such plays be used when you want to surprise the other team or when your team has a numerical advantage near the opponents' goal area.

Defense Against Goal Kick Plays

To defend against goal kicks, your players must try to determine which play the offense will use. If the goalkeeper makes a short pass to the side, attacking players can challenge the ball near the goal. If the goalkeeper kicks far upfield, players can attempt to intercept the ball. The key is for players to communicate, calling out to each other where the ball is kicked and how to defend each play.

Coaching Points for Goal Kicks

1. Direct goal kicks toward the side of the field.
2. Use short, controlled passes to initiate the offense near the penalty area.
3. If the defense pressures the goal kick, pass back to the goalkeeper.
4. Experienced, mature players can surprise attack or take advantage of outnumbering the opponents by kicking the ball downfield.
5. Defend against goal kicks by watching how the offensive team is positioned and by communicating with teammates.

Plays From Indirect and Direct Free Kicks

Direct and indirect free kicks are excellent opportunities for your team to execute set plays to create scoring opportunities. Explain to your players the advantage of these situations.

- Defenders must stay at least 10 yd away from the ball until it is played so that the pass is unhindered.
- The ball is played from a stationary position and therefore is easy to pass.

Remind your players that an indirect free kick must travel forward one full revolution and must be touched by more than one player before a goal can be scored. Set plays from indirect free kicks are used to advance the ball upfield and to attack the goal.

Indirect Free Kick Plays to Advance the Ball

Players have several options to advance the ball from indirect free kicks. Because the ball is far from the opponents' goal, however, your team should protect and control the ball by passing to teammates who are open. Because defensive players must remain 10 yd from the ball, a good play is to have another teammate stand near the ball to receive the pass, then return the ball to the kicker or pass back to another teammate who can initiate the offense (see Figure 11-11).

Fig. 11-11

Indirect Free Kick Plays to Attack the Goal

Two effective options for attacking the goal are to (a) loft passes in front of the goal for headed or volleyed shots (see Figure 11-12) and (b) pass to open players in the penalty area for low passing shots (see Figure 11-13). Lofted passes are difficult to execute effectively, so we recommend you teach them to older, more experienced players only. Demonstrate how to loft passes several feet in front of the goal or to the near or far goalposts. Attacking players should run from slightly outside the goal area to each post and across the goalmouth. The goalkeeper will either go to the ball and leave the goal open or will not follow the ball, leaving the receiver with one less defender attempting to intercept the ball.

Fig. 11-12

If the ball is placed farther from the goal, or if your players are not capable of passing in front of the goal, they can pass to open players in the penalty area. This means players must fake and move away from defenders to get free. Of course, an easy method to free a teammate is to initiate play with a second teammate near the ball, as when advancing the ball upfield. However the ball is played, remind your team that the fewer passes and touches needed to shoot the ball, the less time the defense will have to react to the play.

Fig. 11-13

Plays From Direct Free Kicks

Direct free kicks need not be touched by another player in order to score a goal, because the kicker can shoot directly at the goal. The defense will try to prevent a direct shot by forming a wall as close to the ball as possible, for example, 10 yd away. (Your team should also form a wall against direct free kicks on defense.) Your team now has three possible plays.

1. Your kicker can try to shoot at the goal by (a) kicking at the wall, which will most likely block the ball, (b) lofting or chipping over the wall to an open area of the goal, which could be effective if the goalkeeper leaves too much of the goal unguarded, and (c) curving a shot around the wall to an open area of the goal, which could be effective if the goalkeeper leaves too much of the goal unguarded.
2. Your kicker can make a short pass to another player who is open or who moves toward the goal, using plays from the indirect free kick attack.
3. Your players can attempt to form a wall between the ball and the goal in front of and just to the side of the defensive team's wall. This will obstruct the goalkeeper's view of the ball. Then, as the kicker approaches the ball, your players can run away to allow the shot through the wall (see Figure 11-14).

Fig. 11-14

Defense of Free Kicks

If the attacking team is awarded a free kick within shooting range of your team's goal, your team should form a *defensive wall* between the ball and the goal to help block shots. Generally, the farther from the goal the kick takes place, the fewer players are needed to form a wall. Use the guide provided in Figure 11-15 to form walls when the kick is taken from different areas.

Fig. 11-15

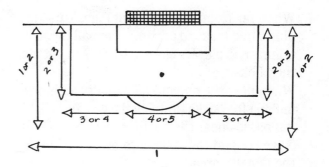

Assign the job of aligning a defensive wall to a competent player other than the goalkeeper. We recommend that you not use your best defenders in the wall, because the wall is designed simply to block the ball, and able defensive players will still be needed elsewhere to guard dangerous offensive players. Players outside of the wall should be instructed to mark free offensive players and to cover specific areas of the field. Be sure to discuss these assignments prior to games and rehearse them in practices. For indirect free kicks within 10 yd of the goal, position all your players in a wall along the goal line.

Assembling the wall can be tricky for young players, so we recommend that you instruct your players to (a) position one player directly between the ball and the goalpost nearest the ball, (b) position one player on his or her outside shoulder, and (c) position other players on the inside shoulder (see Figure 11-16).

Fig. 11-16

Coaching Points for Plays From Indirect and Direct Free Kicks

1. When far from the opponents' goal, use indirect free kicks to advance the ball by positioning two players close to the ball to initiate the offense.
2. When near the opponents' penalty area, use indirect free kicks to attack the goal by (a) lofting passes near the goal for players to head or volley and (b) passing to open players in the penalty area who can shoot.
3. Attacking players should move toward the near or far goalposts and move across the goalmouth.
4. Use direct free kicks to attack the goal by (a) shooting directly at the goal over or around the defensive wall, (b) using an indirect free kick play, or (c) forming an offensive wall or adding to the defensive wall to block the goalkeeper's view.
5. Defend against indirect and direct kicks by forming a wall of players between the ball and the goal.

Plays From Corner Kicks

Corner kicks are excellent opportunities to score goals. Because offensive players cannot be offside, the ball is kicked from a stationary position, and a corner kick can directly score a goal. Your team can use two basic attacks from corner kicks: the *long corner* and the *short corner*.

Long Corner Attacks

Explain that attacking from a long corner means trying to loft the ball either across the goalmouth or to the near or the far goalposts (see Figure 11-17). Demonstrate that goalkeepers will try to catch or punch the ball if played too close to the goal, therefore the players should loft the ball in front of the goal, just out of the reach of the goalkeeper. This way, one teammate can run toward the near goalpost and another can run toward the far goalpost, while a third teammate stands between the goalposts to receive passes

or shoot any loose balls. These plays require an advanced level of skill, so you will need to decide if your players can execute such plays.

Fig. 11-17

Short Corner Attacks

As a surprise play, you can use short corner attacks with players of any age, but they are probably most appropriate for younger players who are unable to kick the ball very far or accurately in front of the goal area. You will only be able to execute this play successfully if the defending team uses fewer than two players to pressure the kick. Remind your players that a defender cannot move closer than 10 yd from the ball, and this will give your players room to execute the play. A typical short corner play is to (a) place two players at the corner, (b) have one player push the ball for the other player (see Figure 11-18) and run in a curve toward the goal, and (c) have the other player dribble until confronted by a defender, then pass to the first player for a shot or pass toward the goal.

Fig. 11-18

The key to defending against corner kicks is how well your players can combine man-to-man and zone defense. Show your players how to mark a player in their zones and play goal side of that opponent to prevent him or her from receiving a pass. If players stand in front to mark, they will not be able to see the movements of that player. The leader for all defensive play near the goal is the goalkeeper. He or she must watch the play develop and direct defensive players to mark opponents and to move around the goal area. A strong, loud voice is a helpful attribute in a goalkeeper.

Coaching Points for Plays From Corner Kicks

1. Use long corners to place the ball out of the goalkeeper's reach in front of the goal or at the near or far goalposts.
2. Place attackers at each goalpost and in front of the goalmouth.
3. Use short corners if kickers cannot effectively pass to the goal.
4. Pass from the corner to players who are open and closer to the goal. These players can cross the ball, shoot, or pass to other teammates.
5. Defend against corner kicks by letting the goalkeeper direct defensive players and by combining man-to-man and zone defensive principles.

Teaching Progression for Set Plays

1. Teach players how to (a) run and circle away from throw-ins, (b) run in and angle away from throw-ins, and (c) throw in and receive return passes from throw-ins.
2. Teach players how to defend against throw-in plays.
3. Teach players how to initiate the offense from goal kicks using (a) short, controlled kicks to teammates near the goal, (b) return passes to the goalkeeper, and (c) long, downfield kicks.
4. Teach players how to defend against goal kick plays.
5. Teach players how to advance the ball from indirect free kicks and how to attack from indirect free kicks.

6. Teach players how to attack from direct free kicks.
7. Teach players how to defend against indirect and direct free kicks.
8. Teach players how to attack from long corner kicks and from short corner kicks.
9. Teach players how to defend against long corner kicks and short corner kicks.

Games and Activities for Set Plays

You have probably noticed that specific activities for set plays were not listed in this chapter. We recommend that you practice the specific plays presented, adding your own unique features. By dividing your team into offensive and defensive units, your team can practice how to execute and how to defend in competitive situations and have fun at the same time.

(11.1) Throw-In Drills
- Run In and Circle Away
- Run Away and Circle In
- Run In and Angle Away
- Throw-In and Receive Return Pass

(11.2) Goal Kick Drills
- Short Control Kicks
- Pass Back to the Goalkeeper
- Long, Downfield Kicks

(11.3) Indirect and Direct Free Kick Drills
- Indirect Free Kicks to Advance the Ball
- Indirect Free Kicks to Attack the Goal
- Direct Shots Into a Defensive Wall
- Lofted or Chipped Shots Over a Defensive Wall
- Curved Shots Around a Defensive Wall
- Indirect Plays From Direct Free Kicks
- Form an Offensive Wall

(11.4) Corner Kick Drills
- Long Corner Attacks
- Short Corner Attacks

Soccer
Planning Guide

Now that you know how to teach soccer skills and offensive and defensive playing strategies, you are probably eager to start the soccer season. But unless you know how to design and conduct practices using the teaching methods and practice activities described in the Soccer Coaching Guide, your enthusiasm could end in frustration. To conduct an effective practice requires careful planning. Take the time to study this Soccer Planning Guide section of *Coaching Soccer Effectively*, and you will find practices more beneficial and enjoyable for your players—and for you.

In this Planning Guide you will find information on your role as a coach and tips to help you work effectively with the young people on your team. Also, you will find information on how to develop long-term seasonal plans and daily practice plans, how to create an environment that will enhance the presentation and practice of soccer skills, and how to evaluate your players' skills and your coaching practices. Just as the Coaching Guide was a practical explanation of how to teach soccer skills, this Planning Guide is a practical explanation of how to conduct effective practices.

In chapter 13 you will find seasonal plans and daily practice plans for three age groups: 6 to 8 years, 9 to 12 years, and 13 to 15 years. These plans include all of the skills needed to play soccer. Skills are taught at a slower rate for younger, less experienced players and at a faster rate for older, more experienced players.

Part III: Coaching the Team

The introduction to the Coaching Guide presented some guidelines to follow for developing your coaching goals and how you would approach your athletes. Now that you are beginning to plan your practices, you need to think about your role as a coach and consider how to actually implement these guidelines.

In this section of *Coaching Soccer Effectively* you will learn about your role as a coach, how to work effectively with players, how to organize your season, and how to develop and conduct daily practice plans. Additionally, you will learn how to prepare your team for their first game, how to evaluate their performances, and how to improve their performances. Lastly, because soccer is a dynamic, flowing game with few breaks, soccer fitness is an important component for preparing your players. Fitness concepts and specific soccer fitness activities are presented for you in chapter 15.

Chapter 12: Understanding Your Role as a Coach

Introduction: Coaching Responsibilities

As a soccer coach you have two distinct responsibilities for coaching young soccer players: (a) to help each player develop soccer techniques and skills and (b) to *combine* skillful players as a team. To do this, you must understand how players learn the game in practice and how your players can apply their learning to actual games. Ensure that your team is ready for game play by structuring practice sessions for the greatest amount of learning and by simulating competitive situations during each practice session. Your practices will prepare the team to play, but the main event is the game. Coaching the team successfully during competitive games is a challenging task.

Getting Started in Coaching Soccer

To coach soccer effectively, you need to understand the nature and objectives of the game and understand key elements in coaching young athletes. If you understand the nature of the game you have the potential to pass on your knowledge

to your players, provide interesting and realistic practices, and manage the team during games. Learning how to coach young soccer players means learning how to pass on your knowledge effectively to the players on your team; this requires an understanding of communication skills. You can learn about these skills by reading the ACEP Level 1 text *Coaching Young Athletes* and by attending an ACEP coaching clinic. Some coaches understand soccer quite well but cannot communicate their knowledge effectively, whereas others do not have great knowledge but are effective communicators. To become an effective coach and really enjoy your coaching experience, try to develop both of these areas. After all, coaching young soccer players should be as fun for you as playing soccer is for young athletes.

Nature of Soccer

Unlike football and baseball, which have many breaks in actual game play, and basketball, which allows fouls and time-outs to influence playing strategy, soccer is a fluid and flowing game with no time-outs and a continual clock. This means that your players must learn to make decisions specific to soccer game play and learn to perform soccer skills. Becoming a proficient player requires years of practice that, for many of your players, begins with you.

Skills and Techniques

Passing, receiving and controlling, juggling, running with the ball, heading, and volleying are examples of skills that your players must practice to play soccer effectively. Simply stated, *skills* are general movements or abilities used to play a sport, *techniques* are specific methods of using each skill. For example, passing is a skill, passing with the inside or outside of the foot is a specific way or technique of performing that skill. Players with poor techniques often perform poorly in games because they have not mastered basic skills and specific techniques.

Learning a broad base of skills and techniques leads to becoming an effective all-around player. Players who concentrate on developing a few specific techniques may not be effective players in games, whereas players who concentrate on developing many techniques and an understanding of soccer concepts will probably be effective players. For example, a high school player, whom we traveled to see, was warming up prior to a game and amazed the crowd with his ability to juggle the ball. We all eagerly awaited his performance in the game. During the game, however, this player was very ordinary and not proficient at controlling the ball when challenged by defenders, or at reacting to the quickly changing conditions of the soccer game. For this player, the juggling was an end in itself rather than a technique to be applied in competitive situations. Coach your players to learn and to develop each skill and technique and to use these abilities in games.

Tactics

Tactics are the methods by which a team achieves its objectives in a game. For players, understanding tactics means selecting the appropriate techniques and skills according to a set game plan. Effective tactical play involves skillful players combining with other skillful players for the best interests of the team. For example, knowing whether to make a long pass or a short pass, at any stage of the game, is a part of tactics. Your offensive tactics may be based around fast forwards, and as a team, you try to pass the ball in the spaces behind the opposing defense for your fast forwards to run into. Your defensive tactics may be based on tall defensive players who are strong headers of the ball, therefore you try to encourage the opposing team to play high balls into your defense. In selecting tactics for your team, look at the strengths of your team and base team play around those strengths.

An effective way of coaching tactical play is to play a scrimmage where you stop the play and point out options to players and focus on decision-making skills. Stop the game and show players how to improve when they make mistakes and also reinforce good play by praising their efforts. Then let them play a game without stopping play, encouraging your players to develop their decision-making skills in an effort to enhance tactical understanding. Many times progress will be slow, but do not get discouraged or frustrated, because these are difficult tasks for young players. Throwing out a list of dos and don'ts is easy but not as effective as focusing on one or two points at each practice and making sure your team learns them well. Covering many points each practice may confuse players.

Decision making depends upon where the play is occurring in relation to the defensive, midfield, and offensive thirds of the field (see Figure 12-1). Use these imaginary thirds to help players make decisions about passing, dribbling, and taking risks. Near their own goals, players should take fewer risks because a mistake could lead to an easy goal by the opposing team. Near the opponents' goal players can afford to take more chances because if the ball is lost, there is plenty of time to recover.

Fig. 12-1

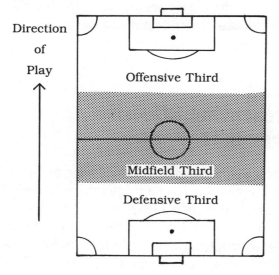

Direction of Play

Offensive Third

Midfield Third

Defensive Third

Fitness

Soccer is a game of constant running and action that requires a high degree of physical fitness. During each game your players will be: (a) jogging and sprinting, (b) involved in body contact with opposing players, (c) continually performing soccer skills, (d) twisting, turning, side stepping, jumping, starting and stopping, and (e) experiencing mental stress from concentration.

As a coach, it is your responsibility to prepare the team for these activities. Much of this preparation will occur in your normal practice schedule in which players work on mastery of technique, skill, tactics, and game play. You may notice from game play, however, that your team is not doing as well as it should in these areas. For example, you may observe that your defenders are not very agile; they are slow turning and starting and stopping. To overcome these problems, structure practice to include activities that develop these abilities. You will find many conditioning activities in chapter 15.

Skills and fitness development for soccer players younger than 13 years should be developed together by combining skills and fitness activities. This will keep the players interested and guarantee that while working on fitness,

they will also be improving their ball skills. When players reach ages 13 to 15 and are serious players, activities without a ball are also appropriate and allow you to focus on specific fitness components.

Principles of Effective Coaching

Coaching soccer involves more than knowing the techniques, skills, tactics, and game of soccer. Many outstanding players are not effective coaches because they are unable to structure learning experiences for players. Think carefully how you can effectively communicate your knowledge to your team by noting the following principles in coaching:

- Motivating players
- Treating players as individuals
- Determining coaching objectives
- Presenting effective demonstrations
- Developing an effective coaching manner
- Analyzing performances

Each of these topics is discussed briefly in this section. However, trying to present all of the components of effective coaching would be inappropriate for this book and would detract from its soccer-specific nature. We highly recommend that you contact your soccer organization or recreation department for information on how you can attend an ACEP Level 1 clinic and learn more about these coaching principles.

Motivating Players

Effective coaches understand how to motivate players by (a) structuring practices that are fun and that keep every player actively involved, (b) setting reasonable but challenging goals that players can accomplish, (c) letting each player experience a reasonable degree of success, and (d) rewarding effort and hustle as well as successful performances. You can implement these points by establishing a player-of-the-week award, rotating team captains each week, and including players in determining personal and team goals.

Treating Players as Individuals

Players have different personalities with contrasting interests and motivations, so you must consider individual differences when coaching players. For example, some players can take more criticism than others without becoming discouraged, whereas others are more sensitive and can only take a little criticism. You will need to be careful with players whom you recognize as being sensitive to criticism and avoid discouraging them. Knowing individual players can even help in selecting players for certain positions and responsibilities. Some players respond to challenges while others feel happier doing things with which they are familiar. By identifying those players who relish a challenge, you can select them to demonstrate skills in difficult practices, because you know they will be prepared for the challenge.

Determining Coaching Objectives

Every practice session should have specific goals and objectives. Objectives are developed from the desired improvements or changes that you hope to achieve with your players. In some cases, the improvements will relate to individual players and to the team in general, but in other cases your major objective may be to increase the knowledge of your players in some aspect of the game. For example, you may notice that your team missed some easy scoring chances, so during the next practice session you specifically plan to practice scoring. On other occasions, your objective will be to improve your team's knowledge

of a rule or tactic such as the offside rule, so you structure the entire practice around this rule. Chapter 14 includes details on how to plan practice sessions.

Presenting Effective Demonstrations

Because players learn by observation and practice, it is better to have a simple and meaningful demonstration than a long, drawn out explanation that is meaningless. Effective demonstrations accomplish two important tasks. First, the players will see a good picture of the techniques and skills to be performed. Second, if players know you are knowledgeable and proficient, they are likely to have faith in what you say. If you feel comfortable demonstrating, go ahead and show your players how to perform. If you have not played much soccer, however, do not worry; demonstrate what you can and use your best players or other skilled players to help demonstrate.

Developing an Effective Coaching Manner

Your manner of communication will affect how your players accept what you have to say. If you are lively and enthusiastic you will probably achieve greater response and effort from players than if you are dull and boring. Several key rules for communicating with players are:

- Use simple language, and approach athletes at their level, not yours. The simpler and clearer your presentations, the more understandable they will be.
- Show enthusiasm and keep your voice upbeat, placing an added emphasis on the most important words. A monotone voice and a lack of enthusiasm can effect your players negatively, while enthusiasm will affect them positively.

- Maintain eye contact with the group. This will show players that you are genuinely interested in them and will also help you determine if your players understand you.

Analyzing Performances

One quality that outstanding coaches share is the ability to analyze their players' performances and to make corrections. This requires the ability to *look into* rather than to *look at* a player's performance. Looking into a performance enables a coach to determine what caused an error and how to correct it, rather than simply spotting the error. Depth in performance analysis takes many years of experience, so if this is your first season, do your best to look for errors and make corrections. Just as your players will improve with practice, so will your ability to coach improve with practice and experience.

Chapter 13: Instructional Schedules and Practice Plans

The Importance of Planning

One of your objectives as a coach is to organize practice sessions with a logical progression of instruction throughout the season. You will need to teach basic ball control skills before you teach your players set plays. This progression from basic skills to advanced skills and tactics involves developing *seasonal plans* of instruction for extended time periods. Another of your objectives will be to organize and plan *individual practices* based upon the seasonal plans and current needs of your team. Coaches must recognize that individual practices require equipment, time management, and organization. Foresighted planning is an essential part of being a coach. This chapter will help you plan effectively by presenting the following topics:

- Developing seasonal plans
- Developing a coaching plan
- Identifying and correcting errors

Developing Seasonal Plans

Before the first practice, you should consider the skill progression you will follow throughout the season to teach your players soccer skills and tactics. Planning your sessions in advance will provide a "road map" or directions for you. Even if you change your original plans, the process is valuable, because systematic planning will help you remain organized. We suggest that, if time permits, you introduce or review all the fundamental techniques and skills during the first several weeks before the first game. As the first game approaches, spend more time on defensive and offensive strategy and set plays during practice games. Also, it is important to evaluate the abilities of your players and to develop a style of play that emphasizes their strengths.

Choose Appropriate Activities

Of course, to do this, you need to decide which skills, techniques, and tactics are appropriate for the players on your team. This process is not clear-cut and depends upon the maturation and experience of each individual player. From our experience, young players within certain age ranges can learn and effectively perform certain skills and enjoy certain activities. We recommend that you follow the guidelines listed below in choosing the skills and activities appropriate for your players.

Age	*Activities*
5-7	Tag and chasing games Individual ball work Opportunities for vigorous play Activities that take a short explanation
8-10	All techniques Enjoy practices with opposition Activities involving cooperative effort Competitive activities
11-13	Introduce basic tactical principles Strong desire to improve skill level Receptive to team organization
14-16	Benefit from full-sided game Able to grasp advanced tactical concepts Trying to develop specialist skills for positions Extremely competitive

Also, we have noticed that although children need specific instruction, they discover and learn many skills on their own, by trial and error, just by playing with the ball. For example, young players often learn to receive, control, and dribble quite effectively in an unstructured setting by playing with friends. Therefore, allow some free play time during practices, rather than filling every moment of each practice with formal instruction and set drills. Small-sided scrimmage games are excellent for providing an unstructured play setting in which players experiment and learn by trial and error. We are not advocating complete free play each practice but providing enough free time for players to experiment,

practice, and learn on their own or with teammates. Teammates are often your best assistant coaches.

Prepare an Instructional Schedule

Developing a teaching schedule for an entire season is difficult, because the needs of each player and of your team will change as the season progresses. We believe that a full seasonal plan is better than none, but it should be flexible enough to change as the needs of players and of your team change. We prefer to develop plans over a 3- or 4-week period, called an *instructional schedule*, that provides direction for the skills, techniques, and tactics to be taught. Changes can be included in the next set of instructional schedules while maintaining long-term direction.

Included below are instructional schedules for players 6 to 8 years (less mature), 9 to 12 years (moderately mature), and 13 to 15 years (more mature). Notice that these schedules cover a 4-week period with two practice sessions each week for a total of eight practice sessions. For most youth soccer leagues, this will be enough time to prepare for your first game. These instructional schedules can be used in their present form, but they are intended to be used as general guidelines rather than as strict plans. Try using them and alter them as needed to meet the needs of the players on your team. After using the instructional schedule, you will be familiar enough with the guidelines to develop your own schedules for the remainder of the season, using the instructional schedule outline in Appendix B.

4-Week Instructional Schedule for Youth Soccer Ages 6-8

Goal: To help players learn and practice the individual and team skills needed to play a regulation game after 4 weeks.

T(10): Teach and practice the skill initially in 10 min.   *: These skills are practiced during the drills
P(10): Review and practice the skill for 10 min.

Skills	Week 1		Week 2		Week 3		Week 4		Time in Minutes
	Day 1	Day 2	Day 1	Day 2	Day 1	Day 2	Day 1	Day 2	
Warm-up Exercises	T(5)	P(5)	P(5)	P(5)	P(5)	P(5)	P(5)	P(5)	40
Cool-down Exercises	T(5)	P(5)	P(5)	P(5)	P(5)	P(5)	P(5)	P(5)	40
Passing/Support									
Short	T(10)							*	10
Long						T(10)			10
Chip						T(10)			10
Drills	P(30)					P(20)	P(10)		60
Receiving									
Wedge		T(10)						*	10
Cushion		T(10)						*	10
Drills		P(10)					P(10)		20
Dribbling									
Ball control									
Against opponents			T(10)						10
Drills			P(30)						30
Heading									
Forward				T(10)					10
Drills				P(30)					30
Juggling									
Foot and thigh		T(10)							10
Scoring									
Shooting					T(10)				10
Drills					P(20)	P(10)			30
Goalkeeping									
Agility							T(10)		10
Handling							T(10)		10
Positioning									
Drills							P(10)		10
Game Play									
Positions								T(10)	10
Full game			T(10)	P(10)	P(10)	P(10)	P(10)	P(20)	70
Small-sided scrimmages	T(10)	P(10)							20
6 versus 4 game drill					T(10)				10

4-Week Instructional Schedule for Youth Soccer Ages 9-12

Goal: To help players learn and practice the individual and team skills needed to play a regulation game after 4 weeks.

T(10): Teach and practice the skill initially in 10 min.   *: These skills are practiced during the drills
P(10): Review and practice the skill for 10 min.

Skills	Week 1		Week 2		Week 3		Week 4		Time in Minutes
	Day 1	Day 2	Day 1	Day 2	Day 1	Day 2	Day 1	Day 2	
Warm-up Exercises	T(5)	P(5)	P(5)	P(5)	P(5)	P(5)	P(5)	P(5)	40
Cool-down Exercises	T(5)	P(5)	P(5)	P(5)	P(5)	P(5)	P(5)	P(5)	40
Passing/Support									
Short	*								
Long		*							
Chip		*							
Drills	P(40)								40
Receiving									
Wedge			T(15)						15
Cushion			T(15)						15
Drills				P(10)					10
Dribbling									
Ball control		*	*						
Against opponents		*					*		
Drills		P(55)	P(10)						65
Heading									
Forward				T(15)	*				15
Backward				T(15)					15
Drills				P(30)	P(10)				40
Juggling									
Foot and thigh									
Scoring									
Shooting	*	*	*		*	P(10)		*	10
Drills							P(30)		30
Goalkeeping									
Agility	*	*	*	*	*	*	*	*	
Handling	*	*	*	*	*	*	*	*	
Positioning	*	*	*	*	*	*	*	*	
Drills									
Offensive Play									
Overlapping	*				*				
Creating space	*				*				
Drills	T(15)				P(30)				45
Individual Defense									
Block tackle						T(15)			15
Containing						T(15)	*		15
Marking						T(15)			15
Drills							P(10)		10
Throw-ins									
Standing							T(5)	*	5
Run and drag							T(5)	*	5
Drills							P(15)	P(10)	25
Game Play									
Positions	*	*	*	*	*	*	*	*	
Small-sided scrimmages			P(15)		P(15)		P(15)	P(30)	75
Full games	P(15)	T(15)	P(15)		P(15)	P(15)	P(20)		95

4-Week Instructional Schedule for Youth Soccer Ages 13 and Up

Goal: To help players learn and practice the individual and team skills needed to play a regulation game after 4 weeks.

T(10): Teach and practice the skill initially in 10 min.   *: These skills are practiced during the drills
P(10): Review and practice the skill for 10 min.

Skills	Week 1 Day 1	Week 1 Day 2	Week 2 Day 1	Week 2 Day 2	Week 3 Day 1	Week 3 Day 2	Week 4 Day 1	Week 4 Day 2	Time in Minutes
Warm-up Exercises	T(5)	P(5)	P(5)	P(5)	P(5)	P(5)	P(5)	P(5)	40
Cool-down Exercises	T(5)	P(5)	P(5)	P(5)	P(5)	P(5)	P(5)	P(5)	40
Passing/Support									
Short	*	*							
Long	*								
Chip									
Drills	P(20)	P(10)							30
Receiving									
Wedge									
Cushion									
Drills									
Dribbling									
Ball control			*						
Against opponents			*						
Drills			P(10)						10
Heading									
Forward						*			
Backward						*			
Sideways						*			
Drills						P(15)			15
Defensive Play									
Tackling		T(15)							15
Individual defense		T(15)							15
Marking and covering		T(20)							20
Team defense				T(15)	(P15)				30
Free Kicks									
Offensive plays			T(15)	P(10)					25
Defensive plays				T(15)					15
Offensive Play									
Shooting					P(20)		P(20)		40
Offensive defense	T(15)								15
Fitness									
Relay						P(15)	P(10)		25
Shuttle						P(15)			15
Drills						P(30)			30
Juggling									
Foot and thigh									
Scoring									
Shooting							P(15)	P(10)	25
Drills			P(15)						15
Goalkeeping									
Agility				P(10)					10
Handling				P(10)					10
Positioning									
Drills									
Diving								T(15)	15
Distribution								T(10)	10
Game Play									
Positions					P(25)				25
Small-sided scrimmages	P(20)						P(20)	P(25)	65
Full game	P(20)	P(20)	P(40)	P(20)	P(20)	P(20)		P(20)	160

Developing a Coaching Plan

A coaching plan developed from the instructional schedule will provide direction for specific coaching sessions. Many experienced coaches, who have years of experience developing coaching plans, may be able to go to practice with ideas in their heads and conduct an effective 90-minute practice. Most inexperienced coaches, however, cannot and should not try this.

The less experienced you are, the more you and your athletes will benefit from your careful planning of each practice. One of the advantages of developing a coaching plan is that the process enables you to become more familiar with the material ahead of time. Often, the plan you write down sticks in your mind so that the plan becomes a mental checklist. Another advantage is that progressions in the practice can be established with careful thought and consideration for player development. In developing your plans, the objective of the coaching session should be kept clearly in mind. Simplicity is a key concept. It is not possible to include every detail on the plan. It is best to note the main points and condense your thoughts into simple phrases and key coaching points.

As with instructional schedules, coaching plans should be flexible enough to change and meet the needs of your players or the conditions

Practice Plan 1

Age: 6-8
Total time: 60 minutes

Instructional Goals
Practice short low passing with effective support play.

Equipment
Balls, cones, jerseys

Drills and Games
Passing—Passing Through Cones Drill
        —Passing Circle Drill
        —Circle Keep-Away Drill
Game—Small-Sided Scrimmage Game

Component/Time	Activity/Drills	Organization	Coaching Points
Introduction Warm-up 5 min	Meet players; check the roster. Stretching and ball gymnastics	Bring the team together. Form a circle for stretching. Supply one ball per player for gymnastics.	Make sure players understand how to stretch. Demonstrate ball gymnastics.
Teach 10 min (15 min)	Teach players how to pass the ball.	Pair up and practice passing.	Show different surfaces of foot: inside, instep, outside.
Practice 10 min (25 min)	Passing Through Cones Drill	Place two cones 3-4 ft apart about 20 ft from each player.	Use inside of the foot first, then instep and outside.
Practice 10 min (35 min)	Passing Circle Drill	Divide into groups of five or six and form small circles.	Practice passing with each foot and encourage accuracy.
Practice 10 min (45 min)	Circle Keep-Away Drill	Use a group of seven or eight and place one player in the middle of a circle.	Wait till the player in the middle challenges before passing.
Game Practice 10 min (55 min)	Small-Sided Scrimmage Game	Divide into two teams.	Stress keeping possession of the ball.
Cool-down/ Evaluation 5 min (60 min)	Review short low passing skills.	Bring the team together. Watch your time; do not drag on.	Let them know time and place of next practice and practice schedule.

of the field. You may notice a major weakness in several players during a practice or note that players do not understand a fundamental tactical concept. Changing the direction of the practice to focus on that point will often be the most effective part of practice.

Components of Effective Practice

Your practices need to be organized so your players learn as much as possible in a limited amount of time. This is achieved by planning practices so there is a progression. Present techniques, skills, and tactics in a logical manner. Specific coaching plans that correspond to the instructional schedules are presented for you. Again, these plans can be used as they are, but should be considered as general guidelines that can be altered to meet the needs of your players. Remember to involve your players and assistant coaches in this process. Assistant coaches will observe some things you cannot, and players will soon recognize the skills they need to develop and the activities they enjoy.

Notice that each practice specifies:

- The *instructional goals* or what you want to accomplish during the practice.

Practice Plan 2

Age: 6-8
Total time: 60 minutes

Instructional Goals
Practice receiving and controlling using wedge and cushion methods.

Equipment
Balls, cones, jerseys

Drills and Games
Receiving—Toss and Receive Drill
　　　　　—Wedge Direction Drill
　　　　　—Receiving and Turning in Threes Drill
Game—Small-Sided Scrimmage Game

Component/Time	Activity/Drills	Organization	Coaching Points
Introduction Warm-up 5 min	Stretching and ball gymnastics.	Form a line for stretching activities. One ball per player for ball gymnastics.	Introduce coaches. State your goals and expectations.
Teach 10 min (15 min)	Teach how to juggle the ball.	Individual	Use laces and thighs for easy control.
Teach and practice 10 min (25 min)	Toss and Receive Drill	Divide in pairs, 10 yd apart.	Cushion the ball by withdrawing and relaxing the surface.
Teach and Practice 10 min (35 min)	Wedge Direction Drill	Divide into groups of three, 10 yd apart.	Wedge ball against ground using inside and outside of foot.
Practice 10 min (45 min)	Receiving and Turning in Threes Drill	Divide into groups of three, 10 yd apart in a straight line.	Absorb speed of ball by withdrawing foot, pivot, and turn.
Game Practice 10 min (55 min)	Small-Sided Scrimmage Game	No goals, count number of consecutive passes. Five passes = 1 goal.	Stress using cushioning and wedging to receive.
Cool-down/ Evaluation 5 min (60 min)	Review receiving and controlling.	Demonstrate receiving. Answer questions and discuss as a group.	Tell the players what they did well.

- The *component and time* needed for each part of practice or whether you teach a new skill, review a previously taught skill, or conduct a scrimmage game. The length for each part of practice is provided.
- The *activities and drills* used to teach and practice.

Notice that the component/time column includes six components from the ACEP Level 1 book *Coaching Young Athletes* that should be included during each practice:

- Warming up
- Teaching and practicing new skills
- Practicing or scrimmaging under competitive conditions
- Cooling down
- Evaluating practices

Although each component is included for each practice session, they will not and should not always follow this order. Warming up helps prepare players for practice and brings the team together as a unit and should always be the first

Practice Plan 3

Age: 6-8
Total time: 60 minutes

Instructional Goals
Practice dribbling to maintain close control of ball and to dribble past opponents.

Equipment
Balls, cones, jerseys

Drills and Games
Dribbling—Dribble Around Cones Drill
—Bee Hive Drill
—How Many Fingers Drill
—Obstacle Course Drill
—Tag Drill
Game—Full Game

Component/Time	Activity/Drills	Organization	Coaching Points
Introduction Warm-up 5 min	Greet your players. Dribble Around Cones Drill	Bring the team together and set up cones for dribbling.	Be prompt and enthusiastic. Dribble using both feet.
Teach and Practice 10 min (15 min)	Teach how to dribble against opponents by using the Bee Hive Drill.	Lay out cones in a 15- × 20-yd area. Players dribble without touching cones.	Dribble with inside and outside of foot. Use small steps and light touch.
Practice 10 min (25 min)	How Many Fingers Drill	Players dribble around coach who holds up fingers. Players shout how many fingers.	Dribble with head up and in a zigzag pattern.
Practice 10 min (35 min)	Obstacle Course Drill	Players dribble around course taking care not to touch markers.	Use sole, inside, and outside of foot to turn.
Practice 10 min (45 min)	Tag Drill	Use "frozen" and "chain" variations in a 20- × 15-yd area.	Encourage players to use side step, step over, and pass fakes.
Game Practice 10 min (55 min)	Full Game	Play a full game and encourage players to dribble.	Coach players when to dribble near the opponents' goal. Point out danger of dribbling near own goal.
Cool-down/ Evaluation 5 min (60 min)	Review the practice.	Discuss as a group.	Be positive and constructive. Compliment hard work and effort. Review areas that need work for each player.

component to every practice session. Similarly, cooling down and an evaluation of the practice help players recover from practice and meet as a unit before leaving and should always be the last component of every practice session. The other components should be placed where most appropriate for each stage of the season. Early in the season, teaching and practicing new skills is more important and should come before practicing previously taught skills or practicing under competitive conditions. As the season progresses, the importance of these components in relation to one another changes and so should their order in practice sessions. Later in the season, you may wish to spend the whole session scrimmaging and focusing on team play. After you have used these practice plans, you will be familiar enough with them to develop your own for future practices based upon your revised instructional schedules. Use the practice plan outline form in Appendix B to develop your coaching plans.

Practice Plan 4

Age: 6-8
Total time: 60 minutes

Instructional Goals
Practice basic heading technique.

Equipment
Soft balls, cones, jerseys

Drills and Games
Heading—Discover the Heading Surface Drill
       —Head Juggle Drill
       —Heading Circle Drill
       —Heading Keep-Away Drill
Game—Full Game

Component/Time	Activity/Drills	Organization	Coaching Points
Introduction Warm-up 5 min	Stretching and juggling	Stretching in a team circle and juggling in pairs.	Check roster and discuss today's practice.
Teach and Practice 10 min (15 min)	Teach proper heading technique using the Discover the Heading Surface Drill.	One ball per player. Each player brings ball to meet forehead with hands.	Watch ball and contact on forehead. Use soft balls.
Practice 10 min (25 min)	Head Juggle Drill	Start with toss, head, catch sequence and progress to consecutive head jugglers.	Lean head back so ball goes up into air.
Practice 10 min (35 min)	Heading Circle Drill	In groups of 4-5 players form a circle. Players head back and forth around circle.	Head through the ball by throwing head at the ball. Use legs to propel trunk, neck, and head to meet the ball.
Practice 10 min (45 min)	Heading Keep-Away Drill	In groups of three, two players try to keep the ball away from the other player.	Head underneath ball to perform high header. Watch ball onto forehead.
Game Practice 10 min (55 min)	Full Game	Divide into two teams and play a regular game.	Use a soft game ball and encourage players to head ball when it is in the air.
Cool-down/ Evaluation 5 min (60 min)	Jogging and stretching	Jog as a group and stretch in a circle.	Provide feedback during cool down. Praise effort and attention.

Using the Activities/Drills

Each activity and drill listed can be found in the drills section of each chapter in this book and in the Drills List on pages xi-xii. If you cannot remember where a drill is located, find that drill in the Drills List and identify the number for that drill. For example, the *Bee Hive* is number 4.2 and is the second drill listed in chapter 4.

Using Coaching Grids

The coaching grid is an area of the field or playing surface divided into squares by cones or other markers, such as shirts or shoes. In one square or groups of squares, games and practices can be organized. In fact, many of the games and activities presented in the Coaching Guide are played in grids. The size of the square is gener-

Practice Plan 5

Age: 6-8
Total time: 60 minutes

Instructional Goals
Practice methods of scoring goals with an emphasis on shooting low and to the corners.

Equipment
Balls, cones, jerseys

Drills and Games
Shooting—Rapid Fire Drill
　　　　—Shooting From a Distance Drill
　　　　—Three versus One to Goal Drill
　　　　—Six versus Four Game Drill
Game—Full Game

Component/Time	Activity/Drills	Organization	Coaching Points
Introduction Warm-up 5 min	Stretching and dribbling	Lead stretches in a circle. Dribbling as a group around field.	Check roster and discuss today's practice.
Teach and Practice 10 min (15 min)	Teach shooting techniques. Then practice by using the drills that follow: Rapid Fire Drill	Players line up at top of penalty area. Serve balls for shots at goal.	Assess the position of the goalkeeper before shooting. Emphasize accuracy before power.
Practice 10 min (25 min)	Shooting From a Distance Drill	Divide into teams of four with two teams at either end of the field. Four defensive players inside penalty area stop four offensive players outside the penalty area from scoring.	Pass to find an opening for a shot. Concentrate on accuracy and shooting low.
Practice 10 min (35 min)	Three versus One to Goal Drill	Six players in a 40- x 20-yd area. Three offensive players try to score against a defensive player and goalkeeper.	Commit defensive player before passing. Create space by spreading out.
Practice 10 min (45 min)	Six versus Four Game Drill	Play in half of the field with six offensive and four defensive players.	Coach good shooting angles and following all shots.
Game Practice 10 min (55 min)	Full Game	Divide into two teams and play regular game.	Stress selecting the best shooting technique and creating space for scoring chances.
Cool-down/ Evaluation 5 min (60 min)	Jogging and stretching	Jog as a group, stretch in a circle.	Be constructive and enthusiastic. Talk about a famous soccer player.

ally 10 x 10 yds, although this is only a general guideline. Smaller or larger squares can be used according to the age of the players. Grids are used for technique, skill, and tactical practice. Using grids offers the following organizational advantages to coaches:

- A large number of players can be actively involved and easily organized in the grids.
- The grid is particularly useful for developing basic technique and skill. By playing in a small area, each player frequently touches the ball, thereby maximizing the opportunity for technique and skill development.

- In these small areas, gamelike situations can be created with a reduced number of people participating.
- The coaching grid presents opportunities to isolate players who are presented with specific tasks. This makes the grid useful for initial learning of a basic technique, such as passing, and to isolate players for correcting and refining skills.

Practice Plan 6

Age: 6-8
Total time: 60 minutes

Instructional Goals
Practice long passing and chipping techniques.

Equipment
Balls, cones, jerseys

Drills and Games
Passing—Passing Long and High Drill
   —Two players in a Grid Drill
   —Knocking Over Cones Drill
Game—Full Game

Component/Time	Activity/Drills	Organization	Coaching Points
Introduction Warm-up 5 min	Stretching and juggling	Stretch in a group circle and juggle in groups of five.	Emphasize stretching slowly without bouncing and use all body surfaces in juggling.
Teach 10 min (15 min)	Teach how to make chip passes.	Assemble in a semicircle for demonstration and explanation.	Emphasize body position.
Practice 10 min (25 min)	Two Players in a Grid Drill	Set players up in a straight line. End players chip ball over middle player.	Pass in air by kicking underneath the ball.
Teach and Practice 10 min (35 min)	Teach and practice long passing using the Passing Long and High Drill.	Two players pass back and forth with long passes.	Use instep or laces to kick ball. Follow through after contact.
Practice 10 min (45 min)	Knocking Over Cones Drill	Divide into two teams; each team attempts to knock down its set of cones.	Emphasize accuracy before power. Contact middle of ball to keep pass low.
Game Practice 10 min (55 min)	Full Game	Divide into two teams and play full game.	Coach long passing and chipping. Stop game to make coaching points from time to time.
Cool-down/ Evaluation 5 min (60 min)	Dribbling	One gentle half lap of field with each player dribbling a ball.	Evaluate the practice. Be positive and constructive.

Practice Plan 7

Instructional Goals
Practice fundamentals of goalkeeping.

Equipment
Balls, cones, jerseys

Drills and Games
Goalkeeping—Ball Handling Exercises
　　　　　—Goalkeeper Agility and Reaction
　　　　　　Exercises
　　　　　—Goalkeeper Shuffle Drill
Shooting—Rapid Fire Drill
Game—Full Game with Modification

Component/Time	Activity/Drills	Organization	Coaching Points
Introduction Warm-up 5 min	Easy stretching and juggling	Stretch in a group circle, juggle individually.	Check roster and review today's practice.
Teach and Practice 10 min (15 min)	Teach handling skills by using Ball Handling Exercises.	One ball per player.	Develop movement first, then increase speed.
Teach and Practice 10 min (25 min)	Teach agility using Goalkeeper Agility and Reaction Exercises.	In pairs, 10 yd apart, players serve balls to each other.	Emphasize holding ball to chest after collecting.
Practice 10 min (35 min)	Goalkeeper Shuffle	In groups of three: Goalkeeper; Shooter; Caller; each other.	Stress goalkeeper adjusting to the changing position of ball and covering the goal.
Practice 10 min (45 min)	Rapid Fire Drill	Shooters line up at top of penalty area and receive a ball served by the coach to shoot at goal. Shooter becomes goalkeeper.	Emphasize positional play with goalkeeper a few feet away from goal line.
Game Practice 10 min (55 min)	Full game with modification	Divide into two teams and play a game where each team attacks two goals. Use cones to form goals.	Rotate goalkeepers in each of the four goals so everyone plays goalkeeper.
Cool-down/ Evaluation 5 min (60 min)	Review skills.	As a group, discuss role of goalkeeper.	Explain importance of learning all the skills of soccer to be an effective player.

Practice Plan 8

Age: 6-8
Total time: 60 minutes

Instructional Goals
Practice key skills of passing and receiving and incorporate into practice games with emphasis on positional play.

Equipment
Balls, cones, jerseys

Drills and Games
Passing—Circle Keep-Away Drill
Receiving—Toss and Receive Drill
Game—Full Game

Component/Time	Activity/Drills	Organization	Coaching Points
Introduction Warm-up 5 min	Stretching and ball gymnastics	Form a circle for stretching. Each player should have a ball for ball gymnastics.	Warm up easily and review today's practice.
Practice 10 min (15 min)	Circle Keep-Away Drill	Use a group of seven or eight and place one player in the middle of a circle.	Wait till the player in the middle challenges before passing.
Practice 10 min (25 min)	Toss and Receive Drill	Divide into pairs, 10 yd apart.	Cushion ball by withdrawing and relaxing surface.
Game Practice 10 min (35 min)	Full Game	Divide into two teams and play regular game.	Concentrate on passing and receiving to keep possession.
Teach 10 min (45 min)	Explain roles of defense, midfield, and offensive players.	Rotate players through positions on field.	Stress general responsibilities of each position.
Game Practice 10 min (55 min)	Full Game	Divide into two teams and play regular game.	Stress good passing and receiving with players in defensive, midfield, and offensive positions.
Cool-down/ Evaluation 5 min (60 min)	Dribbling	One gentle half lap of field with each player dribbling a ball.	Emphasize working as a team and trying hard for team as well as yourself.

Practice Plan 1

Instructional Goals
Practice maintaining possession of ball with good support play.

Equipment
Balls, cones, jerseys

Drills and Games
Passing—Call and Run Drill
　　　　—Circle Keep-Away Drill
　　　　—Give-and-Go
　　　　　or Wall Pass 1 Drill
　　　　—Four versus Four Marking and Covering Drill
Game—Full Game

Component/Time	Activity/Drills	Organization	Coaching Points
Introduction Warm-up 5 min	Meet players; check the roster.	Bring the team together.	Introduce the coaches. State your goals and expectations.
Practice 10 min (15 min)	Call and Run	Divide into groups of five or six in 20- × 20-yd squares.	Receiver moves toward passer to receive ball.
Teach and Practice 15 min (30 min)	Circle Keep-Away Drill	Divide into groups of eight and play in area 30 × 30 yd.	Encourage passes to split defensive players.
Teach and Practice 15 min (45 min)	Give-and-Go or Wall Pass 1 Drill	Offensive players combine with a passer who acts as a wall to beat defensive player.	Stress passing the ball firmly to the wall player, who then redirects the ball.
Practice 15 min (60 min)	Four versus Four Marking and Covering Drill	Divide in teams of four and play game on small field.	Stress possession with good support play.
Game Practice 15 min (75 min)	Full Game	Divide into two teams and play game.	Encourage possession and emphasize support play.
Cool-down/ Evaluation 5 min (80 min)	Review today's practice.	Bring players together.	Be positive and constructive; review principles of support play. Mention time and place for next practice.

Practice Plan 2

Age: 9-12
Total time: 80 minutes

Instructional Goals
Practice skill of beating opposing players with a dribble.

Equipment
Balls, cones, jerseys

Drills and Games
Dribbling—Dribble Around Cones Drill
　　　　—King of the Ring Drill
　　　　—Running the Gauntlet Drill
　　　　—Combat Zone Drill
Game—Full Game

Component/Time	Activity/Drills	Organization	Coaching Points
Introduction Warm-up 5 min	Review the coaches' and players' names.	Bring players together.	Be enthusiastic. Let them know you care about learning skills and having fun.
Practice 10 min (15 min)	Dribble Around Cones Drill	Six cones or markers in a line 6 ft apart.	Dribbling using all foot surfaces.
Teach and Practice 15 min (30 min)	King of the Ring Drill	In a square 15 × 20 yd.	Stress changing direction and shielding ball.
Teach and Practice 15 min (45 min)	Running the Gauntlet Drill	Make a corridor 30 × 10 yd and divide into three squares.	Dribble at the defensive player and fake before dribbling past defensive player.
Practice 15 min (60 min)	Combat Zone Drill	Mark four 10-× 10-yd squares and form an offensive and defensive team.	Use step over and side step fakes.
Game Practice 15 min (75 min)	Full Game	Divide into two teams.	Dribble near opponents' goal. Stress safety near own goal.
Cool-down/ Evaluation 5 min (80 min)	Review key points on dribbling.	Bring players together.	Compliment effort and hustle.

Practice Plan 3

Age: 9-12
Total time: 80 minutes

Instructional Goals
Practice receiving and controlling ball under pressure from opponents.

Equipment
Balls, cones, jerseys

Drills and Games
Dribbling—Dribble Around Cones Drill
Receiving—Quick Control Drill
          —Receive and Control Under Pressure Drill
Game—Small-Sided Scrimmage Game
     —Full Game

Component/Time	Activity/Drills	Organization	Coaching Points
Introduction Warm-up 5 min	Juggling drills and stretching	One ball per player.	Use foot, thigh, chest in juggling sequence.
Review Practice 10 min (15 min)	Dribble Around Cones Drill	Six cones in a line 6 ft apart.	Use both feet and all foot surfaces.
Teach and Practice 15 min (30 min)	Quick Control Drill	In a 10- × 10-yd square one player receives and passes to supporting players to keep possession.	Select wedge or cushion method as early as possible.
Teach and Practice 15 min (45 min)	Receive and Control Under Pressure Drill	In pairs in 10- × 10-yd square. Receiving player controls ball and dribbles to cone.	Practice receiving ball by taking ball to either side away from passer.
Game Practice 15 min (60 min)	Small-Sided Scrimmage Game	Divide players into four teams and play two small-sided scrimmages.	Apply condition of two-touch play with no dribbling.
Game Practice 15 min (75 min)	Full Game	Divide into two teams.	Provide players with information on their methods of receiving and controlling.
Cool-down/ Evaluation 5 min (80 min)	Dribbling	One gentle lap of field each player dribbling ball.	Keep the cool-down easy; review practice during cool-down. Be constructive; mention time and place for next practice.

Practice Plan 4

Age: 9-12
Total time: 80 minutes

Instructional Goals
Practice heading sideways and backward.

Equipment
Balls, cones, jerseys

Drills and Games
Receiving—Quick Control Drill
Heading—Heading Circle Drill
      —Heading Backward Drill
      —Throw, Head, and Catch Drill
      —Headed Goals Only

Component/Time	Activity/Drills	Organization	Coaching Points
Introduction Warm-up 5 min	Dribbling and stretching	Dribble around field. Choose two players to lead stretching.	Warm up easily.
Review Practice 10 min (15 min)	Quick Control Drill	In a 10- × 10-yd square, one player receives and passes to supporting players to keep possession.	Select wedge or cushion methods of control.
Teach and Practice 15 min (30 min)	Heading Circle Drill	Form a circle of five to eight players with one player in the middle.	Stress heading ball sideways by using upper body, neck, and head to redirect the ball.
Teach and Practice 15 min (45 min)	Heading Backward Drill	Form groups of three in a straight line.	Head with a quick backward flick of the head.
Practice 15 min (60 min)	Throw, Head, and Catch Drill	Divide players into two teams in a field 50 × 40 yd.	Both teams use a throw, head, catch sequence to move the ball down the field and to score.
Practice 15 min (75 min)	Headed Goals Only	Play regular scrimmage game with a 10- × 10-yd square on each side of the penalty area.	Offensive players dribble into square, pick up and throw the ball to teammates for a header at goal.
Cool-down/ Evaluation 5 min (80 min)	Jogging and stretching	Choose two players to lead cool-down. Jog as a group. Stretch in a group circle.	Cool down easily. Compliment effort and mention that effort is an important quality of an effective soccer player.

Practice Plan 5

Age: 9-12
Total time: 80 minutes

Instructional Goals
Introduce basic offensive principles.

Equipment
Balls, cones, jerseys

Drills and Games
Heading—Heading Circle Drill
Offense—Three versus One Overlap Drill
　　　—Creating Space in Front of the Goal Drill
Game—Small-Sided Scrimmage Game
　　　—Full Game

Component/Time	Activity/Drills	Organization	Coaching Points
Introduction Warm-up 5 min	Juggling and stretching	Choose two players to lead warm up.	Warm up easily. Discuss today's practice.
Review Practice 10 min (15 min)	Heading Circle Drill	Form a circle of five to eight players with one player in the middle.	Stress heading ball sideways by using upper body, neck, and head to redirect the ball.
Practice 15 min (30 min)	Three versus One Overlap Drill	Three offensive players try to score against a defensive player and a goalkeeper.	Offensive players spread out to create width and one player overlaps from a deep position.
Practice 15 min (45 min)	Creating Space in Front of the Goal Drill	In the offensive third of the field, four offensive players try to score against two defensive players.	Encourage players to attack down flanks by passing ball to outside and then crossing to the far post.
Game Practice 15 min (60 min)	Small-Sided Scrimmage Games	Divide players into four teams and play two small-sided games.	Stress spreading out to create space and attacking with depth.
Game Practice 15 min (75 min)	Full Game	Divide players into two teams and play a full game.	Encourage players to move without the ball into goal-scoring positions.
Cool-down/ Evaluation 5 min (80 min)	Jogging and stretching	Choose two players to lead cool-down as a group. Review the practice during cool-down.	Cool down easily. Review skills that need improvement. Mention time and place for next practice.

Practice Plan 6

Age: 9-12
Total time: 80 minutes

Instructional Goals
Introduce technique of tackling, individual defense, and defense as a team.

Equipment
Balls, cones, jerseys

Drills and Games
Offense—Three versus One Overlap Drill
Defense—Block Tackle Drill
　　　　—Partner Tackle Practice Drill
　　　　—Four versus Four Marking and Covering Drill
Game—Full Game

Component/Time	Activity/Drills	Organization	Coaching Points
Introduction Warm-up 5 min	Stretching and ball gymnastics	Warm up in a circle.	Be enthusiastic. Discuss today's practice.
Practice 10 min (15 min)	Three versus One Overlap Drill	Three offensive players try to score against a defensive player and a goalkeeper.	Offensive players attack with depth.
Teach and Practice 15 min (30 min)	Block Tackle Drill	Two players stand 3 ft apart with a ball between them.	Players attempt to win the ball by challenging with the inside of the foot and knee over ball.
Teach and Practice 15 min (45 min)	Partner Tackle Practice Drill	In a 10- × 10-yd square the defensive player contains the offensive player and tackles to win the ball.	Approach the offensive player and attempt to contain unless there is an opportunity to tackle.
Practice 15 min (60 min)	Four versus Four Marking and Covering Drill	In half of the field use four defensive players to defend a goal against four offensive players.	Stress covering and marking offensive players and anticipation to intercept passes.
Game Practice 15 min (75 min)	Full Game	Divide players into two teams and play a full game.	Emphasize that all players must learn to play defense.
Cool-down/ Evaluation 5 min (80 min)	Juggling	Each player juggles trying to keep the ball off the ground.	Ask players to consider how many times someone dribbled past them? Review the major points of good defense.

Practice Plan 7

Age: 9-12
Total time: 80 minutes

Instructional Goals
To teach techniques and strategies at throw-ins.

Equipment
Balls, cones, jerseys

Drills and Games
Defense—Partner Tackle Practice Drill
Throw Ins—Throw-In Drills
Game—Small-Sided Scrimmage Game
    —Full Game

Component/Time	Activity/Drills	Organization	Coaching Points
Introduction Warm-up 5 min	Stretching and group juggling	Stretch individually and divide into groups of five for juggling.	Stress slow, static stretching. Use foot, thigh, chest in juggling.
Review Practice 10 min (15 min)	Partner Tackle Practice Drill	In a 10- × 10-yd square, the defensive player contains the offensive player and tackles to win the ball.	Approach the offensive player and attempt to contain unless there is an opportunity to tackle.
Teach Practice 10 min (25 min)	Standing and Run and Drag Techniques	Divide into pairs and practice two different techniques.	Standing throw for accurate short passes, run and drag for longer throws.
Teach and Practice 15 min (40 min)	Throw-In Drills	Divide into pairs and start by throwing from a kneeling position.	Throw with both hands from behind head.
Game Practice 15 min (55 min)	Small-Sided Scrimmage Game	Divide into four teams and play two games. When ball goes out of play restart with a throw-in.	Emphasize that a throw-in is a pass and the importance of keeping possession.
Game Practice 20 min (75 min)	Full Game	Divide into two teams and play a regular game.	Encourage players to try different throw-in techniques according to game situations.
Cool-down/ Evaluation 5 min (80 min)	Review today's practice.	Bring players together.	Review rules on throw-ins and explain importance of keeping possession of ball at throw-ins.

Practice Plan 8

Instructional Goals
To practice methods of creating and scoring goals.

Equipment
Balls, cones, jerseys

Drills and Games
Shooting—Shooting in Groups of Five Drill
    —Cut-Throat Drill
Game—Six versus Four Game
    —Small-Sided Scrimmage Game

Component/Time	Activity/Drills	Organization	Coaching Points
Introduction Warm-up 5 min	Stretching and ball gymnastics	Choose two players to lead warm-up.	Warm up easily.
Practice 10 min (15 min)	Throw-In Drills	Divide into pairs and practice throw-ins.	Stress accuracy and throwing in for easy control.
Teach Practice 15 min (30 min)	Shooting in Groups of Five Drill	Divide into groups of five, two players either side of the goal take turns shooting.	Practice shooting using all foot surfaces and concentrate on accuracy.
Teach Practice 15 min (45 min)	Cut-Throat Drill	In the penalty, one player plays against two players and tries to score.	Coach principle of following all shots.
Game Practice 15 min (60 min)	Six versus Four Game	Play in half of the field with six offensive players and four defensive players.	Coach principles of taking the opportunity and determining the best shooting technique.
Game Practice 15 min (75 min)	Small-Sided Scrimmage Game	Divide into teams of three and play small-sided scrimmages.	Coach principles of shooting low and away from the goalkeeper and shooting from a good angle.
Cool-down/ Evaluation 5 min (80 min)	Juggling	Players juggle in pairs trying to keep ball off ground.	Emphasize having fun and trying hard. Mention time and place of game.

Practice Plan 1

Age: 13 and up
Total time: 90 minutes

Instructional Goals
Review offensive play and introduce principles of team offense.

Equipment
Balls, cones, jerseys

Drills and Games
Passing—Circle Keep-Away Drill
Offense—Three versus One Overlap Drill
    —Give-and-Go or Wall Pass 1 Drill
Game—Small-Sided Scrimmage Game
    —Full Game

Component/Time	Activity/Drills	Organization	Coaching Points
Introduction Warm-up 5 min	Introduce yourself and other coaches. Check the roster. Ball juggling and stretching.	Bring players together, then juggle and stretch individually.	Be enthusiastic. Juggle with all body surfaces and stretch without bouncing.
Practice 10 min (15 min)	Circle Keep-Away Drill	Divide into groups of six to eight players with one player in circle.	Stress passing only after defensive players commit themselves.
Practice 10 min (15 min)	Three versus One Overlap Drill	Three offensive players try to score against a defender and a goalkeeper.	Offensive players should spread out to create width. One player should overlap from a deep position.
Teach and Practice 15 min (45 min)	Give-and-Go or Wall Pass 1 Drill	In a corridor 15 yd wide facing toward goal, two players complete a wall pass.	Start with no opposition and progress to using a wall pass against a defensive player.
Game Practice 20 min (65 min)	Small-Sided Scrimmage Game	Divide players in four teams and play two small-sided games.	Coach attacking with depth and spreading out to create space.
Game Practice 20 min (85 min)	Full Game	Divide into two teams and play regular game.	Stress moving with and without the ball and exploiting the One versus One situation.
Cool-down/ Evaluation 5 min (90 min)	Review today's practice.	Bring players together.	Correct skills positively. Mention time and place for next practice.

Practice Plan 2

Age: 13 and up
Total time: 90 minutes

Instructional Goals
Review defensive play and introduce principles of team defense.

Equipment
Balls, cones, jerseys

Drills and Games
Offense—Give-and-Go or Wall Pass 1 Drill
Defense—Partner Tackle Practice Drill
       —Defending From Behind Drill
       —Two versus Two Marking and Covering Drill
Game—Full Game

Component/Time	Activity/Drills	Organization	Coaching Points
Introduction Warm-up 5 min	Review players names, juggle and stretch.	Bring players together, then juggle and stretch individually.	Juggle using foot, thigh sequence and stretch with a ball.
Review Practice 10 min (15 min)	Give-and-Go or Wall Pass 1 Drill	In a corridor 15 yd wide facing goal, two players complete a wall pass before shooting.	Start with no opposition and progress to using a wall pass against a defensive player.
Teach and Practice 15 min (30 min)	Partner Tackle Practice Drill	In a 10- × 10-yd corridor a defensive player contains offensive players.	Emphasize defensive player containing offensive player.
Teach and Practice 15 min (45 min)	Defending From Behind Drill	Divide players into groups of three. Defensive players prevent offensive players from turning with ball.	Stress patience and working to win ball until offensive player attempts to run.
Teach and Practice 20 min (65 min)	Two versus Two Marking and Covering Drill	In a 20- × 30-yd area in front of goal two defensive players defend against two offensive players.	Encourage verbal communication between two defensive players as they mark and cover opponents.
Game Practice 20 min (85 min)	Full Game	Divide into two teams and play a game.	Focus on individual defense and how players mark and cover opponents.
Cool-down/ Evaluation 5 min (90 min)	Review today's practice.	Bring players together.	Be positive; compliment effort and hustle. Provide constructive feedback.

Practice Plan 3

Age: 13 and up
Total time: 90 minutes

Instructional Goals
To practice offensive play at free kicks.

Equipment
Balls, cones, jerseys

Drills and Games
Defense—Beat the Defender Drill
Free Kicks—Indirect Free Kicks to Advance Ball
　　　　　—Indirect Plays From Direct Free Kicks
Game—Full Game

Component/Time	Activity/Drills	Organization	Coaching Points
Introduction Warm-up 5 min	Easy stretching and dribbling	Stretch in a group. Players dribble around field.	Keep the warm-up easy and stress using all foot surfaces in dribbling.
Practice 10 min (15 min)	Beat the Defender Drill	In a 10- × 10-yd corridor an offensive player tries to dribble past a defensive player	Defensive players should move in to reduce space and contain offensive players.
Practice 15 min (30 min)	Indirect Free Kicks to Advance Ball	Let players practice two options: lofted passes and passing to open player.	Stress keeping lofted passes away from the goalkeeper.
Teach Practice 15 min (45 min)	Indirect Plays From Direct Free Kicks	Practice taking shots against a defensive wall.	Practice curving and chipping around and over wall.
Game Practice 40 min (85 min)	Full Game	Divide into two teams and play a regular game, stopping the game and awarding free kicks to both teams.	Let players experiment with different types of free kicks. Encourage improvisation.
Cool-down/ Evaluation 5 min (90 min)	Stretching and gentle dribbling	Choose two players to lead cool-down; stretching as a group, dribbling individually.	Review practice; be positive and constructive. Mention time and place for next practice.

Practice Plan 4

Age: 13 and up
Total time: 90 minutes

Instructional Goals
To practice defensive play at free kicks.

Equipment
Balls, cones, jerseys

Drills and Games
Free Kicks—Indirect Play From Direct Free Kicks
Goalkeeping—Ball Handling Exercises
              —Goalkeeper Agility and Reaction Exercises
Game—Full Game

Component/Time	Activity/Drills	Organization	Coaching Points
Introduction Warm-up 5 min	Stretching and dribbling around field	Choose two players to lead stretching.	Keep warm-up easy. Discuss today's practice.
Practice 10 min (15 min)	Indirect Plays From Direct Free Kicks	Practice taking shots against a defensive wall.	Practice curving and chipping around and over wall.
Teach 15 min (30 min)	Teach players how to form a defensive wall.	Rotate players so all players have fun being part of a defensive wall.	Coach players lining up wall and forming a wall.
Teach 15 min (45 min)	Teach players the basics of man-to-man and zone defense	Practice taking free kicks against both man-to-man and zone defense.	Zone defense: assign players specific areas in front of goal. Man-to-man: assign individual opponents.
Practice 10 min (55 min)	Ball Handling Exercises	One ball per player.	Develop movement pattern first. Then encourage speed.
Practice 10 min (65 min)	Goalkeeper Agility and Reaction Exercises	In pairs, 10 yd apart, players serve balls to each other.	Emphasize bringing the ball to the chest after it has been collected.
Game Practice 20 min (85 min)	Full Game	Divide into two teams and play a regular game, stopping the game and awarding free kicks to both teams.	Stress marking and covering skills in defense. Encourage players to organize quickly once the free kick has been awarded.
Cool-down/ Evaluation 5 min (90 min)	Group juggling	Divide into groups of four or five with one ball. Group tries to keep ball in air.	Emphasize having fun and cooperating as a group.

Practice Plan 5

Age: 13 and up
Total time: 90 minutes

Instructional Goals
To develop an understanding of positional and team play.

Equipment
Balls, cones, jerseys

Drills and Games
Positional Play—Positional Scrimmage Game
Team Defense—Goal Kick Drills
Scoring—Six versus Four Drill
Game—Full Game

Component/Time	Activity/Drills	Organization	Coaching Points
Introduction Warm-up 5 min	Stretching and dribbling around field	Choose two players to lead warm-up.	Warm up easily. Use stretches that involve a ball.
Practice 25 min (30 min)	Positional Scrimmage Game	Divide into two teams and play game.	Stop game three or four times in 10 min to clarify responsibilities of defense, midfield, and offense.
Practice 15 min (45 min)	Goal Kick Drills	Divide into two teams and start game with goal kick. Develop a variety of plays.	Show players different options at goal kicks: start control, pass back to goalkeeper, and long downfield kick.
Practice 20 min (65 min)	Six versus Four Drill	Play in one-half of the field with six offensive and four defensive players plus a goalkeeper.	Organize offensive players according to selected system of play. Experiment with various combinations of midfielders and offensive players.
Game Practice 20 min (85 min)	Full Game	Divide into two teams and play regular game.	Talk to players during game about positioning.
Cool-down/ Evaluation 5 min (90 min)	Individual juggling	One ball per player, let them experiment with different juggling routines.	Review the practice, point out skills that need work and those that have been mastered.

Practice Plan 6

Instructional Goals
To improve fitness levels.

Equipment
Balls, cones, jerseys

Drills and Games
Fitness—Hold Him Back Drill
        —Piggy Back Dribble Drill
        —Competitive Relays Drill
        —Shuttle Runs Drill
        —Circuit Training Drill
Game—Full Game

Component/Time	Activity/Drills	Organization	Coaching Points
Introduction Warm-up 5 min	Stretching with a ball and ball gymnastics	Choose two players to lead warm-up.	Warm up easily. Discuss today's practice.
Practice 10 min (15 min)	Hold Him Back Drill Piggy Back Dribble Drill	In pairs, one player restrains the other. In pairs, one player dribbles a ball with partner on back (a modification of the Piggy Back Passing Drill).	Provide rests between strenuous activity.
Practice 15 min (30 min)	Competitive Relays Drill	In groups of four, organize competitive team relays.	Emphasize dribbling in control.
Practice 15 min (45 min)	Shuttle Runs Drill	In groups of five.	Use work:rest ratio of 1:4.
Practice 20 min (65 min)	Circuit Training Drill	Select five or six skills and set up stations with a distance of 40-50 yd between stations.	Stress sprinting from station to station and performing techniques as fast as possible but correctly.
Game Practice 20 min (85 min)	Full Game	Divide into two teams.	Stress working hard to maintain skill performance.
Cool-down/ Evaluation 5 min (90 min)	Stretching	Choose two players to lead cool-down.	Point out how fatigue influences skill performance. Let them know how hard they worked.

Practice Plan 7

Age: 13 and up
Total time: 90 minutes

Instructional Goals
Practice methods of scoring.

Equipment
Balls, cones, jerseys

Drills and Games
Fitness—Competitive Relays Drill
Scoring—Shoot Out Drill
        —Six versus Four Drill
Heading—Headed Goals Only Drill
Game—Small-Sided Scrimmage Game

Component/Time	Activity/Drills	Organization	Coaching Points
Introduction Warm-up 5 min	Stretching and ball gymnastics	Choose two players to lead warm-up.	Warm up easily. Discuss today's practice.
Practice 10 min (15 min)	Competitive Relays Drill	Run relays with groups of four.	Emphasize controlled dribbling.
Practice 15 min (30 min)	Shoot Out Drill	One at a time, players go one-on-one with the goalkeeper, starting 30 yd from goal.	Encourage controlled dribbling and tell players to decide on shooting past or dribbling around the goalkeeper.
Practice 15 min (45 min)	Headed Goals Only Drill	Divide into two teams and mark a square at each goal. The offensive team places a player in the square.	Player in square picks ball up and throws to teammate in goalmouth for a header.
Practice 20 min (65 min)	Six versus Four Drill	Play in half of field; start with six versus four and progress to six versus six.	Vary number in defense according to skill level of offense. Create a game with plenty of scoring chances.
Practice 20 min (85 min)	Small-Sided Scrimmage Games	Divide into groups of five and play three versus two in 40- × 30-yd area.	Rotate players after 5 min. Teach controlled possession for team of three and fast break for team of two.
Cool-down/ Evaluation 5 min (90 min)	Dribbling around field	Choose two players to lead dribbling.	Review the practice. Mention time and place of next practice.

Practice Plan 8

Instructional Goals
Practice diving, positioning, and distribution for goalkeepers.

Equipment
Balls, cones, jerseys

Drills and Games
Shooting—Shoot Out Drill
Goalkeeping—Dive Progression Drill
                —Throw and Punt Drill
Game—Small-sided Scrimmage Game
        —Full Game

Component/Time	Activity/Drills	Organization	Coaching Points
Introduction Warm-up 5 min	Dribbling around the field; individual stretching	Lead group in dribbling and stretching.	Keep warm-up easy and show players how to use all surfaces in dribbling.
Practice 10 min (15 min)	Shoot Out Drill	One at a time, players go one-on-one with the goalkeeper. Start 30 yd from goal.	Encourage controlled dribbling. Tell players to decide on shooting past or dribbling around the goalkeeper.
Teach and Practice 15 min (30 min)	Dive Progression Drill	Using cones, make small goals, 5 yd wide. Working in pairs, players take turns as goalkeepers.	Teach diving with players starting on knees and progress to crouching or squatting.
Teach and Practice 10 min (40 min)	Throw and Punt Drill	In pairs, practice punting. Release ball from hands and punt to partner.	Kick using laces with a strong vigorous follow-through.
Game Practice 25 min (65 min)	Small-Sided Scrimmage Game	Organize teams of three or four players and one goalkeeper. Goalkeeper initiates play.	Stress accuracy and control for offense and for goalkeeper.
Game Practice 20 min (85 min)	Full Game	Divide into two teams and play regular game.	Rotate goalkeepers every 5 min.
Cool-down/ Evaluation 5 min (90 min)	Group juggling	Divide into groups of four or five with one ball.	Emphasize having fun and trying hard in practice.

Chapter 14: Playing Games and Evaluating Performances

Introduction: Excitement of the Game

Games should be an exciting and enjoyable experience for your players. They will have practiced many hours to learn skills, techniques, and tactics, and this is their opportunity to use these abilities against another team. Similarly, games should be an exciting and fun experience for you. Many coaches, however, under the pressure of the game situation, need to remind themselves that coaching should be fun. In this chapter, we offer suggestions to help you prepare for games, coach during games, and evaluate what to do after games that will increase your enjoyment and the enjoyment of your players.

Pregame Preparation

Preparation for games should begin the last practice just before a game. During this practice, emphasize the playing skills and techniques needed for the positions your players will play, and play a scrimmage game to review playing tactics and set plays. Leave enough time at the end of this practice to discuss the upcoming game with your players. Each player should know the location and time of the game and, if possible, the positions and periods of the game he or she will play. If you have not decided upon playing positions and playing periods at the final practice, do so before arriving at the game. Above all, make this practice fun and end on a positive note.

Players and coaches should arrive at the game site 30 to 45 minutes before the kickoff. This will give you time to organize your team and give your players time to warm up properly prior to the beginning of the game.

- Inspect the field and tell the officials and field supervisor about any dangerous or hazardous conditions, such as large rocks, sprinkler heads, and so forth.
- Prepare a first aid kit, containing ice, towels, water, and Band-Aids.
- Encourage players to warm up by practicing fundamental skills, such as dribbling, passing, shooting, and throwing in.
- Call the team together and review player positions, game strategy, and how the field, wind, sun, and other factors could affect play.

During the Game

Coaching during games is likely to be both fun and frustrating for you. You will enjoy watching players work together, hustle, and make understandable mistakes. You will also get frustrated watching players make the same mistakes over and over and coming close to scoring a goal. This often leads inexperienced coaches to shout instructions or talk to their players throughout the game. Providing occasional instructions is necessary, but talking too much or at an inappropriate time is more of a distraction than a help. Remember, the game is for the players, so provide instruction as needed, but avoid badgering players. When you do talk to your players, provide short, clear, and meaningful feedback. Once the game begins, you can do little to change the course of the game, so you may as well remain relaxed and calm. Consider taking notes and using the evaluation forms provided in Appendix C.

Evaluate your players' performances during the first half, and save most of your comments for halftime. During halftime provide feedback to individual players and to the entire team. Identify strengths and weaknesses of the opponent, and discuss changes that need to be made. Keep your remarks short and simple, focusing on a few important points, rather than many nonessential points. Again, remain positive and encourage players to do their best. If your players are losing but are playing with determination and hustle, let them know they are playing well and that scoring goals will come.

After the Game

The period immediately after the game can be a time of extreme elation or great disappointment for your players, and it is a time when your players are likely to be emotional. Try to remain calm and, if positive comments are not possible, say nothing and wait until a later time when you and your players can be more analytical. Regardless of the outcome of the game, emphasize positive aspects of the game and let players know if they played well. Players who made mistakes may be aware of them and do not need to be reminded. Have a short team meeting after the game to discuss the time and location of the next practice. Keep the meeting brief.

Evaluate Playing Ability

After each game, review players' performances with your assistant coaches. Decide if your team played above, below, or equal to their ability for this stage of the season. Determining what players need to work on may not be obvious, because many coaches rely on their overall impressions of the game. These overall impressions may have focused on one or two positive or negative aspects of play rather than on each component of the team's performance.

We recommend that you use the two coaching aids located in Appendix C: The Team Performance Checklist and the Individual Skills Checklist. The Team Performance Checklist will help you evaluate the quality of team performance by identifying errors and evaluating possible causes for the errors. The Individual Skills Checklist will help you evaluate the ability of each player to perform soccer skills. Make photocopies of these checklists, and use them during practices and games to chart the progress of your team.

Develop Skills

After each game, you will have many ideas about how to structure future practices, about the skills that need to be refined, and about new skills that need to be introduced. Refer to the Soccer Coaching Guide for an analysis of skills, techniques, and playing strategies, and attempt to correct skills and team play as soon as possible. Improvement comes slowly, so you will need to be patient. As your players become more experienced and learn how to work together better, both you and your players will have more fun.

An effective method for improving skills and team play is to structure scrimmages and activities, which have certain restrictions or conditions, called *conditioned games*. You probably noticed several conditioned games in the Coaching Guide, such as no-dribble games or games in which players could touch the ball only once before passing. Conditioned games force players to develop skills they tend to neglect and to work together effectively to protect and to advance the ball.

Identifying and Correcting Errors

This section provides an example of how to identify errors and correct them for skillful soccer play. Included are (a) *an analysis of the problem*, (b) *the coaching objective* or what you want to accomplish, and (c) *a coaching plan* to correct the problem.

Problem: Inability to Maintain Possession of the Ball

Maintaining possession of the ball is an important aspect of team play, because if your team has the ball, the other team cannot score. Also, the longer your team is in possession of the ball, the greater your chances of scoring. If your players' skills are not well developed, keeping possession of the ball is not easy, but it is worth working hard to improve this ability in order to develop effective team performances.

Analysis of Problem

Although the technical skills of passing and receiving are average, the major deficiency is support play. Support play is where players move off the ball to support the player in possession by providing passing angles.

Coaching Objective

Your coaching objective is to improve support play. Players need to understand what support play is and how this relates to being able to keep possession of the ball. Start from a simple situation that clearly shows your players how to support their teammates, and gradually develop practices that provide opportunities to practice support play. The final test is the scrimmage game, where you observe how your players support each other in a game situation and make corrections when necessary.

Coaching Plan

Once you have analyzed the problem and decided on your coaching objective, the next task is to decide what to include in the practice that best addresses your coaching objective. Select practice activities that provide an opportunity to improve support play and that give you an opportunity to coach the important points about support play. The following coaching plan includes the components to accomplish the coaching objective.

Skill and Technique Practice

Before players can support each other, they need to be able to pass the ball, so start the practice with an activity that emphasizes short passes and player movement. Select short passing because it forces players to move to open areas and to support players with the ball, thereby increasing the chances of keeping possession of the ball.

Team Play Practice

After practicing short passes, use activities that reinforce general playing systems, such as conditioned scrimmage games. Begin with limited opposition, and add opposition until players are put under the sort of pressure that they may find in a game situation. Try the following:

1. Play 3 versus 1 in a 10- by 10-yd square with three players acting as offensive players and one player a defensive player. The basic coaching points of support play can be introduced:
   - Support so there is an angle for the pass.
   - Support far enough away from the defender to give you time to control the ball.
   - Move into spaces to support the player with the ball.
2. Play 5 versus 2 in a 20- by 20-yd square with five players acting as offensive players and two players acting as defensive players with the five players trying to keep possession for as long as possible. Change the practice to 6 versus 2, if it is too difficult for the five players to keep possession of the ball.

3. Play 5 versus 2 in a 40- by 30-yd field with small goals. Five players are always on offense and play in both directions. Two players are always on defense and attempt to stop the five from scoring. There are no goalkeepers, so use small goals measuring 5 yd wide. This practice gives intensive practice in keeping possession of the ball to the five players. After 10 minutes, rotate the roles of the players so everyone has a chance to play offense.

Tactical Practice

Practice offensive and defensive tactics in small-sided games of 4 versus 4 or 5 versus 5. With fewer players on each team, the game is simplified and you easily show players how to support each other. Use regular size goals at this stage and work with your goalkeepers on supporting fellow players to keep possession. In the game situation, coach your players to always look to pass the ball forward if they are not under immediate pressure. If they are under pressure, have them pass the ball backward. The next player receiving the ball then looks for a foward pass. This way, players can advance the ball while maintaining control of it.

Conditioned Game

Specify conditions, such as two-touch play, allowing one touch to control the ball and one touch to pass the ball, or no-dribble games that force players to control the ball and to look up to observe the position of teammates and defenders. Change game conditions as players improve.

Scrimmage Game

Play a full-sided game and see how well your players have learned to support each other. Each team is challenged to keep possession of the ball for as long as possible. Keep a record of each team's highest number of consecutive passes without losing possession. Goals can be scored, but reward the team with the best support play by awarding three extra goals to the team with the highest number of consecutive passes. Stop the game from time to time to reemphasize important coaching points. Try *freezing the play*: Stop the scrimmage with players staying in their exact positions when you call "Freeze!" While players are frozen you can show players how to provide better support, move to create space, or spot potential offensive and defensive situations. Remember to recognize players who are playing effectively.

Chapter 15: Fitness for Soccer

Introduction: A Game of Constant Running and Action

Your players will quickly discover that running is an essential part of soccer. They may need to run long distances to set up the offense or to defend. The rapid and constant change from offense to defense, with no time-outs and a continuous clock, makes soccer an action-packed game. As the game continues your players will find that effectively performing soccer skills becomes more difficult because continuous running and repetitive action makes them tired. Therefore, as a coach, you need to be aware of the physical demands soccer places on your players and how to condition them to ensure optimal performance throughout each game.

Physical Demands of Soccer

Although each position requires slightly different techniques and skills, only goalkeepers require fitness training that is significantly different from that of other players. Also, because we recommend that only older players specialize at positions, specific training for goalkeepers should not begin until players are mature. To help you understand the training needed to play soccer, we have outlined the physical demands of soc-

cer play and provided some ideas for developing the physical skills needed to play effectively. For additional information, we recommend reading the physiology section of the ACEP Level 1 textbook *Coaching Young Athletes* or the ACEP Level 2 book *Coaches Guide to Sport Physiology*.

Endurance

Due to the length of the game, the amount of running involved, and the repetitive movements involved in soccer, players must develop sufficient endurance to play throughout a game. The best way to develop endurance is to repeat soccer skills over and over. Running long distances will help players develop cardiovascular endurance and the leg endurance essential to all phases of soccer. Similarly, repeated practicing of dribbling, heading, throwing in, and shooting will help players develop the endurance needed to perform these skills well throughout an entire game.

Strength

Developing endurance will also help players develop strength. In contrast to endurance training, significant increases in strength result when exercises require movement of moderate to heavy resistance for a short period of time or for few repetitions. Players can develop strength using a variety of approaches and equipment. For young players, however, the best approach is to use their own body weight as resistance while performing exercises specific to soccer skills.

Speed

Every player can benefit from improving his or her speed. Unfortunately, speed is not as easy to improve as is endurance or strength. Most improvements in speed will result from your players becoming stronger, reacting faster, and developing the endurance needed to decrease muscular fatigue. In short, to develop speed in players, have them practice performing specific movements as fast as possible and develop all other fitness components.

Power

Power is a combination of strength and speed and is essential to passing, shooting, and jumping. Because power is a combination of two other physical components, the best way to train for power is to combine strength and speed training to pass, shoot, and jump as forcefully and as quickly as possible.

Flexibility

Flexibility refers to the ability to stretch and move the arms, legs, neck, and body through a range of motion. The greater the range of motion, the greater the flexibility. Similar to endurance, flexibility can be improved substantially through repeated practice. Also, the greater the flexibility of a muscle and joint, the more stress that body part can tolerate and the less chance of injury.

Developing Fitness

You can develop these fitness components by devoting a specific part of your soccer practice to fitness training. The time needed to develop these fitness components properly, however, often means eliminating valuable time from developing soccer skills during your weekly or biweekly practice sessions. For most youth teams, a better approach is to take time during practice to demonstrate exercises your players can use to develop fitness components and encourage them to train with friends and family outside of practice. Also, you can use the format of the practice session itself to develop fitness components. Alternating activities that are vigorous and physically demanding with activities that are less vigorous and that allow players to recover follows the *work/rest* principle of training. Similarly, alternating activities that emphasize different fitness components follows the *variation* principle and allows players to train separate components throughout the practice session. The practice plans provided in chapter 13 were developed to provide for the development of soccer skills and the fitness components needed to play soccer effectively by alternating work and rest periods and by varying the fitness components emphasized in each activity.

Purpose of Conditioning for Different Ages

Before planning conditioning drills, carefully consider the age, interests, and abilities of your players. Young players need very few specific conditioning drills and will benefit from developing their skills. If you coach older players, conditioning drills are more appropriate.

Conditioning for Players 6 to 8 Years

Players in this age group are maturing physically and mentally and are probably being exposed to soccer for the first time. They have a high energy level, tire quickly, and have a short attention span. For these players it is more important to practice skills and to use soccer games to gain conditioning benefits. Specific conditioning drills will be of little value. Plan a variety of activities that exercise different body parts to prevent injuries. Limit these activities to 10 minutes per practice session.

Conditioning for Players 9 to 12 Years

Many players in this age range will have previous soccer experience, but some will be playing soccer for the first time. Although these athletes also are developing physically and mentally, they have longer attention spans and do not tire as easily as younger players. Consequently, practice activities should be used to capture their interest and to provide conditioning. Some older players in this age range, however, may be ready for advanced skills and may need additional conditioning. For these players, consider using many of the exercises listed in this chapter that would help them become better skilled and physically fit for soccer.

Conditioning for Players 13 to 15 Years

Players in this age range have probably made a more serious commitment to playing soccer than younger players and enjoy practicing and playing games. Many of these players will want to train hard, both at practice and on their own, to improve their soccer skills. Although most of the time spent at each practice should still focus on teaching and practicing skills, you can include more intensive conditioning in several ways.

- Design practices to be more thorough and longer in duration.
- Save the last 10 to 15 min of each practice session for fitness activities.
- Assess individual conditioning needs depending upon the athlete and the positions played.

Additional Fitness Activities

(15.1) Interval Running

Interval running involves running a moderate-to-fast pace for a given distance or time, alternated with rest or light activity, and is an excellent method of developing endurance and leg strength. Select shorter or longer distances depending on which type of endurance you are trying to develop, but remember that intensive training is not effective for young athletes, so hold back on long, hard training until your

players are 13 years and older. Excessive training may "burn out" young athletes who are interested in having fun and learning how to play soccer.

(15.2) Shuttle Runs

Shuttle runs develop endurance and strength and are an excellent way to condition older, more experienced players. We advise they not be used for young, beginning players. Organize players in groups of three with a ball or cone serving as a marker at 10-, 20-, and 30-yd intervals. The first player in each group runs to the first ball and back to the start, to the second ball and back, and to the third ball and back. The second player then performs the same sequence, then the third player does. In this example, players are working one third of the time and resting two thirds of the time, with a work to rest ratio of 1:3, providing an adequate training effect for most young players. If your players become tired quickly, form teams of five players to create a work to rest ratio of 1:4. Then, you can decrease the work to rest ratio as the season progresses and your players become more fit.

(15.3) Competitive Relays

Competitive relays accomplish the same goals as interval training and will be enjoyed by your players because they are races. Use relays with teams of varying numbers of players to develop fitness qualities. Organize relays with and without a ball or a combination of movements with and without the ball. An example of a relay is presented in Figure 15-1 and proceeds as follows:

Divide your team into three or four equal groups, with one ball per group. Mark a starting line and a turn-around line 15 to 20 yd apart. Position players in lines along the starting line. Each player in front of the line dribbles to the turn-around line and back, passes the ball to the next player on his or her team, and moves to the back of the line. Each player repeats until every player has completed the run once or the specified number of times.

Fig. 15-1

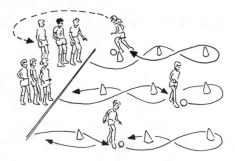

(15.4) Circuit Training

A circuit consists of a number of stations where different soccer techniques are performed. Players move quickly between stations and only rest long enough to regain their breath (see Figure 15-2). Soccer techniques are performed at each station for between 30 and 120 seconds, depending on the intensity of the activity. Organize the players as individuals, pairs, or groups to match the type of activity performed, and even make the circuit competitive by asking the players to keep score for activities such as dribbling in and out of cones, passing between cones, passing to knock over cones, and ball juggling. Demand good quality techniques and keep these activities fun.

Fig. 15-2

(15.5) Hold Him Back

In pairs, one player holds on to the hips of the second player who attempts to sprint forward while being restrained. The restrained player is allowed to run a specified distance, across the penalty area for example, and the roles are reversed. As an alternative, use a towel or belt to restrain the player.

(15.6) Piggy Back Passing

In pairs, one player carries a partner on his or her back for 15 to 20 yd. Match players according to size and weight, making sure each player is capable of carrying the other. Players change roles after the sprint. A variation is *Fireman Dribble*, in which two players carry a third player. These activities can also be used as competitive relays.

(15.7) Chase the Ball

Speed is important in playing soccer, and your players must be able to move as fast as possible while controlling the ball. This practice activity is designed to improve speed with and without the ball. Pair up players as one passer and one chaser, with one ball per pair. Position these teams of two along a sideline. Passers kick the ball forward at least 10 yd, indicated by a marker such as a cone or ball, while the chasers run after the ball and dribble it back. Alternate passers and runners, and repeat. Each time a team is first to advance the ball to the starting line, it scores one point. Play to 10 points.

(15.8) Ball Gymnastics

Ball gymnastics refers to activities involving coordination and agility with a soccer ball. Quite often the activities themselves are never used in the game, but their value lies in the development of coordinated and agile movement. Each player needs a ball for these activities. You can show these activities to your players and ask them to practice in their own time.

Milk Shaker
Stand with the ball in front of the feet, as in Figure 15-3. Jump over the ball with both feet from front to back and from side to side.

Fig. 15-3

Spanish Tap Dance

With the ball in front of the feet, the sole of the left foot touches the top of the ball (see Figure 15-4). Quickly change feet so the sole of the right foot touches the ball. This sequence is continued with each sole touching the ball in turn. Develop a rhythm the pace of which can be of varied. Instruct players not to place all their weight on the ball but to lightly touch the top of the ball. This activity can be used to progressively develop touch control by dragging the ball backward, forward, or sideways with the sole of the foot each time the ball is touched.

Fig. 15-4

Circle Around Body

Sitting on the ground, legs straight with the ball at the feet, roll the ball completely around the body and feet making a wide circle around the body. This stretches the lower back and back of the leg.

Ball Over Head

Sitting on the ground, "pinch" the ball between the feet, lift the ball off the ground and take it back over the head (see Figure 15-5). After the ball has touched the ground behind the head, hold for 10 seconds before bringing the legs back to the ground and sitting upright. This stretches the back of the legs.

Fig. 15-5

Figure Eight

Stand with straight legs at least shoulder width apart. Make a figure 8 by using the hands to roll the ball on the ground around both feet. This movement stretches the back of the legs.

Part IV:
Appendices

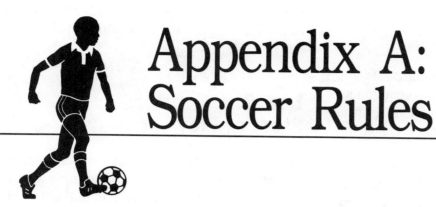

Appendix A: Soccer Rules

Official soccer rules are determined and provided by the Fédération Internationale de Football Association (FIFA), headquartered in Zurich, Switzerland, and these rules govern most national and all international competitions. Sport organizations such as the YMCA of the USA, Soccer Association for Youth, and American Youth Soccer Organization have modified FIFA rules to meet the needs of youth soccer players. Check with your local soccer organization for the rules specific to your league.

The rules presented below are condensed versions of the 17 FIFA Soccer Laws and are intended to provide you with the basic soccer rules in a simplified format. They are not intended to replace any official rulebook adopted by any national or local organization. Where discrepancies exist, you should refer to the official rule book of your league or organization and consider it authoritative.

Law 1:
The Soccer Field

The field of play must be between 100 and 130 yd long and between 50 and 100 yd wide. (These dimensions can be modified as described in chapter 1 for young soccer players.) The field is divided in half lengthwise by the halfway line and has a center circle 10 yd in diameter in the middle of the field. A goal is located at each end of the field and is 8 yd long and 8 ft high. A goal

area 20 yd long and 6 yd deep from the goal line is located directly in front of the goal. A penalty area 44 yd long and 18 yd deep from the goal line is located in front of the goal. Corner arcs with a radius of 1 yd are located at each corner of the field.

Law 2:
The Soccer Ball

Official FIFA soccer balls must be between 27 and 28 inches in circumference, should weigh between 14 and 16 ounces, and should be inflated to between 9 and 10.5 pounds per square inch. Smaller balls such as the #3 ball (circumference 23.5 to 25 inches; weight 10 to 12 ounces), and the #4 ball (circumference 25 to 26.5 inches; weight 12 to 14 ounces) can be used for younger players.

Law 3:
Number of Soccer Players

Regulation soccer games are played with 11 players to a side: 10 field players and 1 goalkeeper. Games must be played with at least 7 players on a side. Substitutes can be used, but no more than 2 during each game. The number of players on a side, number of players needed to continue play, and number of substitutions will vary according to your local league rules.

Law 4:
Players' Equipment

Players should wear clothes that are safe and consistent within a team. The usual equipment consists of a jersey, shorts, shin guards, knee-length socks, and shoes. Shoes are the most important piece of equipment for safety. Shoes that have metal studs or sharp cleats cannot be used. Goalkeeper's must wear clothes different in color from those of the field players on his or her team. Goalkeepers often wear long-sleeved shirts, gloves, kneepads, and elbowpads to protect themselves.

Law 5:
The Referees

The referee is the official in charge of the game. In regulation games one referee monitors play, keeps official time, stops play, allows substitutions, and interprets and enforces all rules. The referee is in complete control of the game and all decisions made by the referee are final.

Law 6:
Linesmen

Linesmen help the referee officiate soccer play. One linesman is assigned to each side of the field to determine when balls are out of play and which team is awarded throw-ins, goal kicks, and corner kicks. Actually, linesmen are extensions of the referee and should be respected just as is the referee.

Law 7:
Duration of Soccer Games

Regulation soccer games last for two halves of 45 min each with a 5 min halftime period. The half-time period will be longer for most youth soccer leagues as long as the league and the referee allow it.

Law 8:
Start of Play

Before play begins, a representative of each team participates in the coin toss to determine which team kicks off and on which end of the field it will play. The team that wins the toss can choose either the end of the field or the kickoff. Teams alternate field sides and kickoff after halftime. At kickoff and all other kicks, the ball is in play after it has traveled its circumference.

Law 9:
Ball In and Out of Play

The ball is always in play as long as it is within the touchlines and goal lines or is touching the lines. The ball is out of play only when it completely crosses playing field boundaries. Because the position of the ball determines in and out of play, players can stand outside the field and touch the ball inside the field.

Law 10:
Scoring Goals

Goals are scored by legally passing the ball across the goal line within the goalposts. If neither team has scored a goal or has scored the same number of goals at the end of a game, a *draw* or tie is declared.

Law 11:
Offside

At least two defensive players must be between an offensive player and the goal at the time the ball is played toward the goal. One of the defensive players can be the goalkeeper. This rule prevents offensive players from standing in front of the goal waiting for the ball. If an offensive player is offside the opposing team is awarded an indirect free kick.

Players cannot be declared offside if they are dribbling the ball or receiving a goal kick, corner kick, throw-in, or dropped ball. In addition, a player will only be called offside if he or she is seeking to gain an advantage by his or her position in the opponents' end of the field.

Law 12:
Fouls and Misconduct

Players who intentionally

- kick or attempt to kick an opponent,
- trip an opponent,
- jump at an opponent,
- charge at an opponent in a dangerous manner,
- charge an opponent from behind,
- strike, spit at, or attempt to strike or spit at an opponent
- hold an opponent
- push an opponent
- touch the ball with the hands

are penalized by awarding the opposing team a direct free kick.

Players who intentionally:

- play dangerously,
- charge a player when not going for the ball,
- obstruct an opponent when not going for the ball,
- charge the goalkeeper who does not have the ball, or
- take more than four steps with the ball when playing goalkeeper

are penalized by awarding the opposing team an indirect free kick.

Players who play dangerously or intentionally try to hurt other players are shown a yellow card as a warning and a red card as judgment to leave the game. These decisions are at the discretion of the referee.

Law 13:
Free Kicks

Free kicks are when players are allowed to kick the ball with defenders at least 10 yd away from the ball. Indirect free kicks must be touched by another player before crossing the goal line into the goal and cannot be kicked directly into the goal. Direct free kicks can be kicked directly into the goal without touching another player.

Law 14:
Penalty Kicks

If a player commits a foul that leads to a direct free kick (see Law 12) inside the penalty area, then the opposing team is awarded a penalty kick from the penalty spot (12 yd directly in front of the goal). During a penalty kick, the offensive player shoots for goal with one touch and only the goalkeeper can attempt to save the ball. The goalkeeper must stand on the goal line.

Law 15:
The Throw-In

A team that last touched a ball that goes out of play along the side of the field loses possession to the opposing team. The opposing team must restart play from the spot the ball went out of bounds by throwing in the ball. Players must hold the ball with both hands and throw the ball over the head while keeping both feet on the ground. Incorrect throw-ins result in the ball being awarded to the opposing team.

Law 16:
Goal Kicks

Balls that go out of bounds beyond the goal line and are last touched by the offensive or attacking team are restarted by the defensive team. The defensive team restarts play with an indirect free kick from within the goal area called a goal kick. The ball must travel outside of the goal area before players from either team can touch the ball.

Law 17:
Corner Kicks

Balls that go out of bounds beyond the goal line and are last touched by the defensive team are restarted by the offensive team. The offensive team restarts play with a corner kick from within the corner arc on the side from which the ball went out of play. The corner kick is similar to a direct free kick, so defensive players must remain at least 10 yd from the ball until it is touched and travels its circumference. The player taking the corner kick cannot touch the ball a second time unless it has been touched by another player.

Appendix B:
Instructional
Schedule and
Practice Plan
Outlines

4-Week Instructional Schedule for Youth Soccer

Goal: To help players learn and practice the individual and team skills needed to play a regulation game after 4 weeks.

T(10): Teach and practice the skill initially in 10 min.   *: These skills are practiced during the drills
P(10): Review and practice the skill for 10 min.

Skills	Week 1 Day 1	Week 1 Day 2	Week 2 Day 1	Week 2 Day 2	Week 3 Day 1	Week 3 Day 2	Week 4 Day 1	Week 4 Day 2	Time in Minutes
Warm-up Exercises									
Cool-down Exercises									
Passing/Support									
Receiving									
Dribbling									
Heading									
Juggling									
Scoring									
Goalkeeping									
Offensive Play									
Defensive Play									
Throw-Ins									
Game Play									

Practice Plan #___

Age: _____
Total time: _____ minutes

Instructional Goals

Drills and Games

Equipment

Component/Time	Activity/Drills	Organization	Coaching Points

Appendix C: Team Performance Checklist and Individual Skills Checklist Outlines

Individual Skills Checklist

Practice (game) _____

Evaluate skills as: Good, O.K., Needs work

Name	Passing	Receive/ Control	Shooting	Heading	Dribbling	Individual/ Defense Tackling	Comments

Team Performance Checklist

Game _____

Evaluate skills as: Good, O.K., Needs work

Team Play	Good	O.K.	Needs Work	Additional Comments
Offensive play				
Defensive play				
Play at free-kicks				
Play at goal kicks				
Play at throw-ins				
Goalkeeping				
Effort				
Attitude				
Communication				

Appendix D:
Coaching Soccer Effectively
Reader
Evaluation Form

Tell Us What You Think

It is our commitment at ACEP to provide coaches with the most complete, accurate, and useful information available. Our authors, consultants, and editors are continuously searching for new ideas and are constantly seeking to improve our materials. Now that you have read and studied this book, it is your turn to tell us what you liked and did not like about it. Please take a few minutes to complete the following survey and send it to: ACEP, Box 5076, Champaign, IL 61820.

Book Evaluation for *Coaching Soccer Effectively*

Instructions: For each statement mark the spaces in the left-hand column that correspond to what you think of this book. We are interested in your opinions so feel free to mark more than one response to each statement.

1. The organization of this book
   ____ (a) presents material in an easy-to-understand progression
   ____ (b) is helpful
   ____ (c) is confusing

2. The material presented in this book is
   ____ (a) easy to read and understand
   ____ (b) difficult to read and understand
   ____ (c) too simple
   ____ (d) too complex

3. Figures and illustrations are
   ____ (a) helpful
   ____ (b) distracting
   ____ (c) technically correct
   ____ (d) technically incorrect
   ____ (e) confusing

4. Coaching points and teaching progressions
   ____ (a) highlight material in the book well
   ____ (b) progress from basic to advanced concepts
   ____ (c) are helpful
   ____ (d) are distracting
   ____ (e) are too repetitive

5. Drills
   ____ (a) need illustrations
   ____ (b) are helpful
   ____ (c) are confusing
   ____ (d) are too advanced for beginning players
   ____ (e) are too simple for beginning players
   ____ (f) are easy to use
   ____ (g) are difficult to use

6. Instructional schedules are
   ____ (a) helpful
   ____ (b) easy to understand
   ____ (c) difficult to understand

7. Practice plans are
   ____ (a) helpful
   ____ (b) confusing
   ____ (c) too basic
   ____ (d) too advanced
   ____ (e) easy to use
   ____ (f) difficult to use

8. Coaching aids are
   ____ (a) helpful
   ____ (b) not helpful
   ____ (c) easy to use
   ____ (d) difficult to use

Yes or No
____ **9. I feel more knowledgeable about coaching soccer to beginning athletes than I did before reading this book.**
____ **10. I would like to attend a workshop or clinic covering the material presented in this book.**

Glossary

Ball out of play: When the entire ball passes beyond the touchline or goal line.

Baseball throw: To throw the ball with an overhand motion, like throwing a baseball. Goalkeepers throw long distances using a baseball motion.

Block tackle: Blocking the ball with the foot to take it from an offensive player.

Bowling throw: To throw the ball with an underarm motion. Goalkeepers throw with a bowling motion to nearby teammates.

Center circle: The circle with a 10-yd radius in the middle of the field. Kickoffs begin here. All defensive players must remain outside of the center circle during kickoffs.

Center spot: The center of the center circle. The ball is started here during kickoffs.

Central forwards: Forwards who play near the center of the field.

Changing direction: To alter the direction of dribbling, such as from forward to sideways to backward.

Chip passes: Passes in the air that rise quickly and drop after a short distance.

Collecting: To catch and control the ball with the hands. Goalkeepers collect the ball after shots.

Controlling: To maintain possession, advance, and maneuver the ball.

Corner kick: A kick from the corner arc awarded to the offensive team because the defensive team has last touched a ball that went out of play beyond their goal line.

Corners: Areas of the field where the endlines and touchlines meet. A 1-yd arc is drawn from this corner to indicate where balls must be placed during corner kicks. Flags are placed at each corner to indicate the area.

Creating goals: Passing the ball around the goal, moving around the goal without the ball, and creating space around the goal for the purpose of shooting the ball at goal.

Creating space: Moving away from defenders or teammates to provide enough playing area to receive passes, shoot, or pass to teammates.

Crossbar: The bar that forms the top of the goal between the goalposts.

Curved passes: Passes in the air that curve to reach a target.

Cushion: To receive the ball by slowing it with the feet or the body.

Defenders: Players nearest their goal who defend the goal from attacks by offensive players.

Defense: Playing against the team controlling the ball and attempting to stop that team from advancing the ball and scoring.

Defensive wall: Aligning defensive players side by side to form a wall between the ball and the goal during free kicks.

Deflect: To push the ball in another direction. Goalkeepers deflect shots by pushing the ball away from the goal.

Direct free kick: A free kick from which a goal can be scored directly, without touching another player.

Dominant foot: The foot a player prefers to use when passing or dribbling because that foot provides the best ball control.

Dribbling: Advancing the ball by pushing it with the feet.

Drop ball: Restarting play by dropping the ball between two opposing players. This can be used after player injuries if no foul has been committed.

Endline (goal line): The lines marking the width of the playing field, from side to side.

Fedération Internationale de Football Association (FIFA): The international organization that establishes soccer rules and play.

Flooding zones: When more offensive players than defensive players move into a zone, the zone is flooded with offensive players.

Following shots: To move in the direction of the ball after shooting.

Forehead: The area of the head, above the eyebrows and near the hairline, where the ball should be contacted when heading.

Forwards: Players nearest the opponents' goal who try to score goals.

Fouls: Any infraction of soccer rules. Major fouls result in direct free kicks and minor fouls result in indirect free kicks.

Fullbacks: Defenders who play near the goal.

Funnel: To move close together near the goal. Defenders move closer together or funnel when near the goal area.

Game halves: The time periods for each game. Each game lasts for two halves of a specified time period.

Goal: The 8-yd long by 8-ft high box at each end of the field through which the ball must pass to score. Also the term used to indicate the number of scores.

Goal area: The 20-yd by 6-yd box marked around the goal and the marked area nearest the goal.

Goalkeepers: Players positioned inside the goalbox who block shots to the goal. Goalkeepers are the only players who can use their hands to control the ball.

Goal kick: Restarting the game by having the goalkeeper kick the ball from inside the goal area.

Goal mouth: Area directly in front of the goal or the opening into the goal.

Goal posts: The posts on each side of the goal that reach to the ground.

Halfway line: The line that divides the field in half from side to side or from touchline to touchline.

Heading: Using the head to play the ball from the air. Players pass the ball by heading it.

Horizontal plane: The area of the ball from side to side.

Indirect free kick: A free kick that must be touched by one additional offensive or defensive player before a goal can be scored.

Inside of the foot: Part of the foot along the arch used to kick the ball.

Instep (laces): Top of the foot used to kick the ball.

Juggling: To keep the ball in the air using the feet, thighs, head, or other body parts, excluding the hands.

Kickoff: When offensive players initiate play inside the center circle by kicking the ball. The ball must roll the length of its circumference before another player can touch it.

Lofted passes: Passes in the air that travel long distances and are less controlled.

Man-to-man: *See* One-on-one.

Mark: To guard or defend offensive players.

Midfielders: Players in the middle of the field who support their teammates on offense and defense.

Nondominant foot: The foot a player does not prefer to use when passing or dribbling because that foot provides the least ball control.

Offense: Controlling the ball against the opposing team and attempting to score goals.

Officials: The people who control the game, calling fouls and balls out of play and awarding goals.

Offside: When the ball is passed to an offensive player positioned near the goal without at least two defensive players between the offensive player and the goal.

One-on-one: When one offensive player is marked or guarded by one defensive player. Also called man-to-man.

Outside of the foot: The outer part of the foot used to kick the ball.

Pass fakes: To pretend or feint a pass to play the ball in another direction.

Passing: To direct the ball by kicking, heading, or throwing.

Penalty area: The 34-yd by 18-yd box marked around the goal. This area also surrounds the goal area.

Penalty area arc: The 10-yd arc on top of the penalty area. All players must stay behind this arc during penalty kicks.

Penalty kick: A direct free kick at goal awarded to the offensive team when the defensive team fouls inside the goal area.

Penalty mark: The spot 12 yd from the center of the goal line. Penalty kicks are taken from here.

Pitch: The soccer field.

Playing systems: The playing formation or position alignment of the defenders, midfielders, or strikers. Examples are the 4-2-4 system, 4-3-3 system, and 4-4-2 system.

Punting: To drop the ball from the hands and kick it in the air.

Ready position: Standing with the legs about shoulder width apart, slightly bent and relaxed, and ready to move in either direction.

Receiving: To gain control of the ball after a pass.

Restarts: Beginning the game after a goal is scored, a foul is committed, or the ball goes out of play.

Rocking throw-in: Standing with the feet in front to back position for the purpose of rocking backward and forward to throw the ball with more power.

Round arm throw: To throw the ball over the top of the body with a sidearm motion. Goalkeepers throw long distances using a round arm motion.

Run-and-drag throw-in: Running and dragging the rear foot to throw the ball with more power.

Running with the ball: Using quick touches with the feet to control the ball while running.

Shin guards: Protective equipment worn inside the socks to protect the shins.

Shooting angle: The straight line between the ball, defenders, and the goal area. This is the direction the ball should be shot at goal.

Short passes: Controlled passes to teammates that do not travel far.

Sideline (touchline): The lines marking the length of the playing field, from goal to goal.

Sidestep: To move from side to side in a shuffle motion, without crossing the feet.

Skills: General movements or abilities. Passing and receiving are examples of soccer skills.

Slide tackle: Sliding into the ball to take it from an offensive player.

Soccer fitness: The physical readiness to play soccer. Soccer fitness involves endurance, strength, speed, power, and flexibility specific to the positions played.

Standing throw-in: Standing with both feet together when throwing the ball into play.

Stopping: To cease advancing the ball in order to pass or change direction.

Strikers: Another name for forwards.

Support play: The nature of soccer play when players help teammates, move into position to receive passes, and control the ball.

Tackle: To stop the ball and take it from an attacker by blocking it with the feet, legs, or body.

Tactics: The playing methods a team uses to accomplish its objectives.

Techniques: Specific methods of using each skill. Passing with the inside and outside of the foot are examples of passing techniques.

Throw-in: Restarting the game by having a player throw the ball into play from outside the field along the touchline into the field.

Turning: Changing direction while maintaining control of the ball with the inside, outside, or sole of the foot.

Vertical plane: The plane dividing the ball into right and left halves.

Wedge: To receive the ball by trapping it between the ground and a foot.

Wings: Forwards who play along the sides or touchlines of the field.

World Cup: Soccer tournament held every four years that includes soccer teams from every country.

Zone defense: Marking and guarding players who enter particular areas or zones of the field.

Index